PROF. DROUU'S CAREER COMPASS:
NAVIGATING YOUR PATH AFTER CLASS 12TH

Dr. Akshita Bahuguna
Dr. Rajesh Naithani

Chennai • Bangalore

CLEVER FOX PUBLISHING
Chennai, India

Published by CLEVER FOX PUBLISHING 2023
Copyright © Dr. Akshita Bahuguna, Dr. Rajesh Naithani 2023

All Rights Reserved.
ISBN: 978-93-56483-14-9

This book has been published with all reasonable efforts taken to make the material error-free after the consent of the author. No part of this book shall be used, reproduced in any manner whatsoever without written permission from the author, except in the case of brief quotations embodied in critical articles and reviews.

The Author of this book is solely responsible and liable for its content including but not limited to the views, representations, descriptions, statements, information, opinions and references ["Content"]. The Content of this book shall not constitute or be construed or deemed to reflect the opinion or expression of the Publisher or Editor. Neither the Publisher nor Editor endorse or approve the Content of this book or guarantee the reliability, accuracy or completeness of the Content published herein and do not make any representations or warranties of any kind, express or implied, including but not limited to the implied warranties of merchantability, fitness for a particular purpose. The Publisher and Editor shall not be liable whatsoever for any errors, omissions, whether such errors or omissions result from negligence, accident, or any other cause or claims for loss or damages of any kind, including without limitation, indirect or consequential loss or damage arising out of use, inability to use, or about the reliability, accuracy or sufficiency of the information contained in this book.

CONTENTS

Preface .... *iv*
Introducing Prof. Drouu .... *vi*
Author's Note.. *viii*

Chapter 1. Catch-22.. 1
Chapter 2. Turache? Turache!!!... 31
Chapter 3. Discover Your *"Self"*... 36
Chapter 4. Find Your True North 57
Chapter 5. Entrepreneurship as career 150
Chapter 6. Courses for Career Options............................... 157
Chapter 7. Higher Education Institutes 196

PREFACE

Are you feeling overwhelmed and confused about your career options after Class 12th? Do you feel like you're stuck in a Catch-22 situation, torn between following your dreams and choosing a career that provides financial stability? Are you struggling to identify your strengths, passions, and interests? Do you feel like you're lacking the necessary guidance and support to make informed career decisions? If you answered yes to any of these questions, then Prof. Drouu's Career Compass is the book for you.

Prof. Drouu's Career Compass: Navigating Your Path After Class 12th is not just another book on career guidance. It is a journey of self-discovery, a roadmap to finding your true north, and a guide to unlocking your full potential. This book will not only help you navigate the complex world of career planning but also empower you to make informed decisions that align with your passions and aspirations.

Through this book, you will learn how to discover your unique strengths, interests, and values. You will explore different career options and gain insights into the skills and qualifications required for each field. You will also learn about entrepreneurship as a viable career option and the courses and higher education institutes that can help you achieve your career goals.

Meet my Student Shivi, a Class 12th student who was struggling to find his career path. Shivi was passionate about music but felt pressured by his parents to pursue engineering. He was torn between following his heart and pleasing his parents. After consulting me, Shivi realized that he could combine his love for music and engineering by pursuing a career in sound engineering. He found a course that aligned with his interests and is now pursuing his dream career. My guidance and career coaching helped Shivi overcome his pain points and unlock his full potential.

If you feel like you're in Shivi's shoes, unsure of which career path to take and feeling torn between your passions and family expectations, don't worry. You're not alone. As a career coach, I've helped countless Class 12th students navigate these challenges and find the path that's right for them.

In Prof. Drouu's Career Compass: Navigating Your Path After Class 12th, I share my years of experience and expertise to guide and inspire you on your career journey. From discovering your true self to finding your true north, this book covers everything you need to know to make informed decisions about your future. And with chapters on entrepreneurship as a career option, courses for career options, and higher education institutes, you'll have all the tools you need to succeed.

But this book is more than just theory. It's rooted in real-life struggles and success stories, like Shivi's, who found a way to combine his passions with my guidance. So whether you're feeling lost, uncertain, or just need a little direction, this book is for you.

INTRODUCING PROF. DROUU

The pen name used by **Dr Akshita Bahuguna** and **Dr Rajesh Naithani** when they write together on careers

Prof. Drouu is an accomplished duo of authors, who are passionate about education, entrepreneurship and career coaching. Their latest book, which is their second collaboration, reflects their extensive experience in the field of education and career guidance.

Dr. Akshita Bahuguna is an Edupreneur and a passionate scholar with innovative ways of teaching and learning. She founded FutureIcons, an educational enterprise that aims to educate youth, enhance their skills, and empower future generations. She has wide-ranging experience in career guidance, educational training, teaching, and mentoring entrepreneurs. Dr. Bahuguna has authored numerous research papers on education and entrepreneurship and is a mentor with FIED, IIM Kashipur, and visiting faculty in many universities across India.

Dr. Rajesh Naithani is an institution in himself. He has been a board member of several international companies and has been a key advisor to Education Minister Dr Ramesh Pokhriyal "Nishank" for the past eleven years. Presently, he is the Vice Chancellor of Himalayiya University, Dehradun. Dr. Naithani is a medicinal chemist with more than 20 years of experience and has been involved in strategy management, marketing, and communications. His vision of making students skilled and employable led him to initiate various small and big educational and skilling centers in Uttarakhand.

Together, as Prof. Drouu, they bring a unique blend of academic expertise and practical experience in education and career guidance. They aim to empower individuals to make informed decisions about their careers and achieve their full potential. Their latest book is a testament to their passion and dedication to making a positive impact in the lives of students and professionals.

AUTHOR'S NOTE

Dear Reader,

Welcome to "Prof. Drouu's Career Compass: Navigating Your Path After 12th Grade." I'm thrilled to be your guide on this journey of self-discovery and career exploration.

This book is a continuation of my previous work, in which I provided professional advice on selecting a career and college after 10th grade. In this book, I delve deeper into the intricacies of choosing a career path, assisting students in navigating the confusion that frequently comes with this decision.

The book's design assists students in determining their true north, examining their alternatives, and discovering their passions. I provide a roadmap through a series of chapters that discuss conflicting thoughts, personal stories, and career choices to assist you in navigating the challenges of selecting a career.

But let me explain what sets this book apart. I, Prof. Drouu, am the one who provides the advice and guidance, and I am a frog. I understand this may appear unusual, but hear me out. Just as a frog emerges fresh from the muck and filth of a swamp, this book assists students and parents in emerging from confusion and finding a career that is right for them.

And that's not all. The book is not your average career guide, which provides "tried and tested" paths. Instead, it encourages you to explore the "Road Less Travelled" and discover your own path. As someone who has made mistakes and learned from them, I share everything I've discovered during my journey of self-exploration and guidance with my students.

From identifying your passions and purpose to exploring your potential and personality, this book covers all of the essential factors that go beyond just hard work. And as you read, you'll discover that this book isn't just for students, but also for anxious parents who are seeking guidance on their child's future.

So, if you're prepared to identify your ideal career choice and explore the road less travelled, join me, Prof. Drouu, on this voyage of self-discovery. Let's dive into the swamp of confusion and emerge with a new outlook on the future.

Best regards,
Prof. Drouu

Chapter 1

CATCH-22

Have you ever felt like you were at a crossroads, uncertain which direction to take? This feeling can be particularly overwhelming for students in class 12 who are faced with the daunting task of making a career choice. The pressure to choose just one path can lead to a Catch-22 situation, where students feel trapped between two contradictory options, each with its own set of advantages and disadvantages.

As a career coach, I have seen many students struggle with this decision-making process. They feel overwhelmed by the vast array of options available to them and often don't know where to turn for guidance. It's not uncommon for them to feel like they're in a hopeless situation, stuck between a rock and a hard place.

But here's the truth: making a career choice is not a permanent decision. It's important to remember that every choice is an interim process that can be undone and changed. Even if you've already chosen a path, there's always room to pivot and pursue an alternative option if your current one isn't working out.

Let me share with you the story of one of my former students, Ria. She was an exceptional student who always excelled in school. Ria opted for science with PCMB in 11th grade and pursued a bachelor's degree in Physiotherapy. She then prepared for masters abroad but later found that the job she landed in that field did not give her the contentment she was seeking. After two years on the job, she started working in the insurance industry and made a career in that field.

Ria's story is a clear example that a student can always change their choice. Every choice is an interim process that can be undone and changed. The key is to remain open-minded and to keep exploring your potential and passions.

As a student, you may be wondering about your future career growth. Let me share an incident that happened with a friend of mine named Koki, who had been feeling stuck in her job for years. She had been trying everything to get a promotion but with no success. When she came to me feeling frustrated and discouraged, I asked her a simple question: "If you were only allowed to possess one advantage over your colleagues to secure a promotion, what would it be?"

She responded with a long list of things, but the most significant advantage for promotion was a vacant position. Even if you possess exceptional skills, knowledge, and a strong work ethic, without an available senior role, the chance for promotion is unlikely. Therefore, the key to career growth is not exclusively about being the best at one's profession but being in the right place at the right time.

The incident teaches us that we should be prepared for opportunities as they dance with the one who is already on the dance floor. So, instead of worrying about where the opportunities are, focus on preparing yourself for them. Remember that career choices can be re-evaluated, and alternative paths can be pursued at any time in your career journey.

In this book, I will provide you with insights and strategies to help you navigate the career decision-making process. We will explore the differences between a dilemma and a Catch-22, and why it's important to recognize the nuances between the two. I will also share with you some common pitfalls to avoid when making a career choice, as well as some best practices for approaching the decision-making process.

Making a career-related choice can be a challenging task, but it's important to understand that every choice is not permanent and can be changed with the passage of time and experience. Don't feel limited by the choices you make early in life. Instead, remain open-minded, explore your potential and passions, and be prepared for opportunities that may present themselves. It's never too late to make a new choice and start a new chapter in your career journey!

Making career decisions can be a unsettling task, especially for students who are faced with a myriad of choices. The terms "Catch-22" and "dilemma" are often used interchangeably, but they have some fundamental differences. A dilemma is a situation where a person is presented with multiple choices, each with its own set of advantages and disadvantages. In the context of career-related dilemmas, individuals may have to choose between multiple career options, each with its own set of pros and cons. The purpose of a dilemma is to consider multiple perspectives of the situation to promote more complex thinking about career choices. An essential aspect of a dilemma is that it fosters analysis and discussion to gain knowledge that can influence the final decision.

On the other hand, a Catch-22 is a paradoxical situation where a person is trapped between two contradictory choices, making it impossible to make a decision. In the context of career decisions, a Catch-22 can occur when a person is faced with a choice between two options, each of which may lead to undesirable outcomes. For example, a student may want to pursue a career of their dreams abroad but is scared of staying alone, or they may find their passion in a field that has limited career options in the future. On the other hand, they may have the option to pursue a more lucrative career, but it may not align with their interests and passions.

The transition from class 10th to 11th was comparatively easy, as school provided options and students needed to choose among them. However, the choices made after class 12th can have a significant impact on a student's future. Few options have contradictory alternatives, giving rise to catch-22 situations. It's important to note that making significant career decisions can be challenging, but it is essential to approach these decisions with a clear mind, consider all the options, and take help from career coaches, mentors, or counselors if necessary. Ultimately, the decision should be based on the student's interests, passions, and long-term goals, and they should not be swayed by societal pressure or external influences.

Choosing a path after class 12 can be a unnerving task, especially when there are multiple options to choose from. To make things worse, the information available to students can often be biased, coming from parents, school, peers, and even neighbors. In India, students are under immense pressure to pick just one path, which can lead to making the wrong decision.

For instance, take the case of Rishav, who had studied science in class 11th and 12th. After completing his 12th grade, he was interested in pursuing BBS, but his father had a different plan for him. His father wanted him to follow in the footsteps of his boss, who had completed his B.Tech from IIT and MBA from another premium institute. The father drew a parallel between Rishav's alignment towards science and his boss's educational background, which led to confusion for Rishav. However, with the help of career coaching, the father's compass was set to a scale of success rather than following someone else's path.

The topic of career coaching is not just limited to students, but also applies to parents as well. In India, there is a common belief that Science is the most prestigious career path, while Commerce and Humanities are often looked down upon. This way of thinking is narrow-minded and fails to acknowledge the existence of alternative, non-conventional career options that may be more suitable for individual students. Fortunately, this book offers many such options in later chapters.

One of the consequences of this traditional mindset is that students often fear making the wrong decision, as they are taught that their choice is permanent and cannot be changed. However, it is important for students to explore their interests and personalities in order to make an informed decision. To create a desirable and fulfilling career path, students should gather unbiased information and make choices based on their own interests and skills, rather than just what is considered prestigious by others. It's important to remember that there is no "one size fits all" approach, as every student is unique and requires a unique solution.

In the next two chapters, we will delve into strategies for creating a desirable career path that aligns with each individual's unique interests and skills. However, before we can do that, we must first address the dilemmas and catch 22 situations that commonly arise in the career coaching process. This chapter will identify these common dilemmas and provide practical solutions for resolving them. By surfacing these problems and providing guidance on how to resolve them, we can help students and parents make more informed decisions about their career paths.

Catch 22
A Pragmatic Path or Following The Dreams:

The dilemma of choosing between a pragmatic path or following one's dreams is something that many students face, especially in the Indian education system. From a young age, students are told that certain professions such as engineering, medicine, and accounting are the only way to success and a better life. The pressure to conform to these set pathways can either make or break students, as some thrive in these fields while others are left unfulfilled.

The issue lies in the fact that following one's passion or choosing an unconventional career path is still not fully accepted in Indian society. Many view it as a lot of hard work with little reward or simply relying on luck. This mindset can lead to confusion and stress for students who feel torn between choosing a secure but unfulfilling path or pursuing their passion despite the potential challenges.

To address this dilemma, it's important to provide students with unbiased information about all available career paths and options. Students should be empowered to make their own choices based on their individual interests, skills, and goals. Whether it's following a pragmatic path or pursuing their dreams, students should have the necessary knowledge and direction to make an informed decision.

Science or commerce or humanities or vocational

The age-old dilemma of students deciding on what stream to choose after their 10th grade has been a subject of concern for many years. The three primary streams of Science, Commerce, and Humanities, along with Vocational studies, present a plethora of choices to students, leaving them in a state of confusion.

But what if we told you that the solution to this problem is to do some "reverse engineering"? Yes, you read it right! Before you decide on the stream, you should first understand yourself and identify your dreams and aspirations. Once you have done that, it's time to calculate the steps to reach your goal.

For example, if you have a dream of serving people, you need to ask yourself some questions. What is it about serving people that attracts you? What are your strengths and weaknesses? What is your personality like? Once you have answered these questions, the next step is to combine your self-knowledge with your dream and mark a path for yourself.

This process of combining your strengths and your dreams, and customizing your career path accordingly, is what we call the "hybrid" approach. By building a hybrid for yourself, you can create a unique path that matches your personality and aspirations.

Gone are the days when students had to limit their choices to the traditional streams of Science, Commerce, and Humanities. The world is changing, and so are the career options. Students can now choose from a wide range of unconventional career paths that suit their interests, skills, and passions.

So, the key to making the right choice is to understand yourself, identify your goals, and build a customized path for yourself that suits your personality and aspirations. With this approach, you can pave the way for a fulfilling and successful career.

Enjoy teenage life or work hard for the future:

To enjoy teenage life or work hard for the future, this is one of the biggest dilemmas faced by students. They are constantly being told to work hard and secure their future, while also being told to live in the present and enjoy their youth. The older generation tends to have a more traditional outlook on life, where they believe that working hard now will lead to a better future. They desire a sense of safety and financial security, and believe that material possessions will bring them happiness. On the other hand, the younger generation has a more carefree attitude, and values experiences and personal fulfillment over material possessions. They believe that following their dreams and desires is the key to happiness.

But for students who are still figuring out what they want to do, it can be difficult to choose between the two. The key is finding your own balance, and understanding that life is not just about working hard and accumulating material possessions, but also about living in the present and enjoying the journey. It is important to set goals for the future, but not at the expense of missing out on the experiences and opportunities that the present has to offer.

Ultimately, it's about finding a balance that works for you. It's okay to work hard and have ambitions for the future, but it's also important to enjoy the present and pursue what brings you happiness and fulfillment. So, don't be afraid to take a step back, assess what you truly value, and create a plan that works for you. After all, life is about finding a balance between working hard and enjoying the ride..

Drop a year or grasp what's in hand:

At some point in a student's life, they may be faced with a difficult choice: take a break and wait for a better opportunity or take advantage of what is currently in front of them. It's a common dilemma, and one that can be difficult to navigate. One such student, Manish, came to me with this issue. Manish was a good student who had completed 12th grade with a 93% score and had taken admission in B.Com Honors in a good college in the University in the Capital. However, during his three years of college, he developed a keen interest in psychology, which he wanted to pursue further.

The problem was that many people had told him that changing his career path was impossible and that finding a job was more important. Additionally, if he wanted to pursue psychology, he would need to take a year or two off to study the subject from scratch and prepare for entrance exams for higher studies. This dilemma left Manish confused and unsure about what to do.

As his mentor, I advised him to do some research and ask himself a few questions. I suggested that he research both the career options, the one in a big company and the one in psychology. This research would provide him with a clearer image of the type of job both options would offer. After his research, I told him to ask himself one simple question: "Why?" Why should he go for the former option or why the latter? The importance of this question is to know what his priorities are and what he truly seeks in life.

After much contemplation, Manish chose to pursue his interest in psychology, taking a gap year to study and then entering a good college. He currently works as a child counselor in a well-known school.

But what if he had gone for the campus placement job? Would that have been the wrong choice? No, it wouldn't have been a wrong choice. If he had gone for the job even after doing all the research and questioning, it would have been because he wasn't sure of his interest or due to different priorities. However, even then, his choice wouldn't have been wrong. Why? Simply because a job would have provided him more exposure to not only his field but also the working environment involved. Additionally, he would have gained more experience and even learned new skills. And if he wished to go for psychology after a few years of working? He always could, as no career choice is the 'end' choice.

In conclusion, the best solution to this dilemma is to do thorough research and ask oneself some important questions. It's important to consider one's priorities and what they truly seek in life. This will help one make a well-informed decision and be happy with it in the long run.

The subject versus college dilemma:

Ah, the age-old question: what subject and college to choose after high school? It's a decision that can shape the course of your life, and it's no wonder that many students find themselves grappling with this dilemma.

Let's take a closer look at this subject versus college dilemma. On the one hand, your choice of subject is critical because it sets you on a certain path toward your desired career. You want to choose a subject that you're passionate about and will enjoy studying for the next several years. On the other hand, the college you choose is equally important because it's where you'll spend a considerable amount of time and where you'll grow and develop as a person.

But what if you find yourself in a situation where you're not able to get the subject you want in the college of your choice? This is a common predicament that many students face. One student I know was in this exact scenario, having been admitted to one of the best colleges in the Capital, but the subject was not to his liking. He felt stuck and unhappy, and eventually dropped out after his second year.

But then there's the other student I know who wanted to study English honors but wasn't able to get admission in any college. She opted for distance learning instead and even went on to get a master's degree in the same subject. She found studying to be immensely enjoyable, but she did miss out on some of the benefits of going to a regular college. Due to the lack of interaction and exposure, she felt that she lacked confidence and the same level of connectivity as her peers who went to college.

What can we learn from these two examples? Well, the bottom line is that both students faced their own unique difficulties, regardless of the choice they made. However, it's also essential to note that both of them sought a sense of satisfaction from their choices. This is the key factor to consider when making such a significant decision. You want to choose the option that will bring you a sense of fulfillment and happiness, both in your studies and your overall college experience.

So, when faced with the subject versus college dilemma, take a deep breath and remember to do your research, consider your priorities, and most importantly, follow your heart. In the end, it's your own satisfaction that matters the most, and whichever choice you make, it'll be the right one for you.

College in home town v/s College in a New City:

Are you one of those students who are trying to make a tough decision between studying in their hometown or going to a new city? Fear not, as we will help you understand the pros and cons of both options and provide you with a logical explanation that will help you make an informed decision.

Let's start with studying in your hometown. One of the biggest advantages of this option is that you do not have to worry about household chores, such as cooking or laundry. Your parents will take care of these things, allowing you to focus on your studies. Furthermore, studying in your hometown gives you a sense of safety and familiarity since you are already familiar with the environment. However, one of the downsides is that there are limited opportunities for exploration and growth, which can limit your potential. Additionally, you may become too dependent on your family and fail to learn self-management skills.

On the other hand, choosing to study in a new city can offer several benefits. First, you will learn how to be independent and self-reliant, which will help you in your future endeavors. You will also learn self-management skills and develop a sense of discipline, which is crucial for success. In addition, studying in a new city will expose you to new environments, opportunities, and networks, enabling you to reach greater heights. However, it can also be challenging since you will be far away from your family, and it may take time to adjust to a new environment.

Both options have their advantages and disadvantages, and the decision should depend on various factors affecting your life. These factors include your parents, passion, personality, potential, and purpose. Your decision should be influenced by these factors, as they will help you make a balanced decision that is in your best interest.

So, in conclusion, carefully weigh the pros and cons of both options and consider the 5P's before making a final decision. Keep in mind that this decision is subjective, and the right choice may differ for each individual. Choose the option that will provide you with the most opportunities for growth and development, while keeping in mind your personal needs and preferences.

Academics v/s Extracurricular

Finding the balance between academics and extracurricular activities is a common challenge that students face. It can be tough to manage the rigorous demands of schoolwork alongside the fun and engaging activities that extracurriculars offer. However, it's important to remember that neither of these aspects should be ignored, as both are critical to building a well-rounded and successful future.

Academics, of course, are at the forefront of a student's educational journey. Your grades and academic achievements can often determine your future opportunities, from college admissions to job prospects. Excelling academically is a crucial step to building a strong resume or curriculum vitae (CV). A CV is a detailed record of your educational and professional background and is typically used for job applications. A strong academic background reflected on your CV will undoubtedly make a positive impact on potential employers.

On the other hand, extracurricular activities such as sports, clubs, and social events can help build character and develop essential skills. These activities can reflect positively on a student's profile, which is a more holistic representation of an individual's achievements and experiences. Your profile includes all aspects of your life that define who you are, including your personal interests, passions, and skills. This information can be helpful in showing colleges and potential employers that you are a well-rounded individual who can bring unique perspectives and experiences to the table.

In summary, excelling in academics and participating in extracurricular activities can both benefit a student's future. While academics can help build a strong CV, extracurriculars can help create a unique profile. Ultimately, it's important to strike a balance between both and find what works best for you.

Loan v/s Leave

As students navigate the path to higher education, they are often faced with a daunting question - loan or leave? With the rising cost of tuition and the ever-increasing burden of student debt, it's no wonder that many students find themselves at a crossroads when it comes to making decisions about their education.

Admission to a top-notch institution is a coveted achievement, but the financial aspect of pursuing higher education can be overwhelming. Many students are forced to consider the tradeoff between taking on substantial loans to fund their education or potentially having to forego their dreams of attending the institution of their choice.

It's a tough choice to make - on one hand, taking out a loan can provide immediate relief, allowing students to cover their expenses and pursue their academic goals. However, the burden of repayment can be a daunting prospect, as students may be required to pay back significant sums of money over an extended period of time.

On the other hand, leaving an institution due to financial constraints can be disheartening, leaving students feeling like they've missed out on a potentially life-changing opportunity.

But what if we told you that there is a third option? Many institutions offer a variety of financial aid options, including scholarships, grants, work-study programs, and more. These options can help alleviate the financial strain of pursuing higher education and provide students with a path towards achieving their academic goals without taking on excessive debt.

It's important to remember that the decision to pursue higher education is a significant one, and it's one that shouldn't be made lightly. By carefully considering all available options and weighing the pros and cons of each, students can make an informed decision that will set them on the path to success.

Whether you choose to take out a loan, seek out financial aid options, or pursue alternative educational opportunities, remember that the pursuit of knowledge is a noble and worthwhile endeavor. So take heart, stay focused on your goals, and remember that with hard work and determination, anything is possible

Professional v/s Academic course:

Choosing between a professional course and an academic course is a common dilemma that students face. Both courses offer a unique set of advantages, and one should choose the course based on their interests and future goals.

An academic course is typically research-intensive, focusing on thesis writing, and reading. It is best suited for individuals who want to pursue a career in teaching, research, writing, or become a professor. An academic course provides in-depth knowledge about a subject area and helps students develop analytical and critical thinking skills. This course provides a strong foundation in theory and concepts, which is essential for those who want to make a significant contribution to the field.

On the other hand, a professional course is more skill-oriented and job-ready, making it an excellent option for students interested in management, engineering, fashion designing, hospitality, medical, and other fields. A professional course is designed to prepare students for the practical aspects of the job market. These courses focus on developing practical skills, industry knowledge, and training on how to implement theories in real-life situations.

In order to make the best choice between these two courses, it's important to consider your interests, goals, and career aspirations. Choosing a course that aligns with your interests can motivate you to perform well and achieve success in the field. Additionally, choosing the right course can help you build a strong foundation that will set you up for future growth and success.

In conclusion, the decision to choose between an academic and professional course depends on the individual's personal goals and career aspirations. It's essential to weigh the advantages and disadvantages of each course, considering your interests, potential, and goals. Ultimately, both courses offer unique benefits and can lead to a fulfilling and rewarding career.

Convincing parent v/s getting convinced:

As students transition into adulthood, they often face the challenge of making crucial life decisions, and one of the most significant ones is deciding on a career path. Parents or caregivers have a significant influence on their children's decision-making process, as they seek to provide the best possible future for them. However, this influence can sometimes put a lot of pressure on children or hinder them from pursuing their interests.

Let me illustrate this dilemma with two stories of my former students. The first student, Fayth, was unsure of her career goals after completing 10th grade. Despite her love for reading, she opted for commerce stream, which proved to be a challenge, and she struggled to perform well. However, after 12th grade, she convinced her parents to let her pursue a degree in English literature, which was her true interest. Although she still has no clear career goal in mind, she continues to pursue her passion for learning, writing, and studying, and has a Masters's degree in English, with plans to pursue a Doctorate.

In contrast, my second student didn't know what she wanted to do, but her parents recognized her potential in accounting and suggested that she pursue Chartered Accountancy (CA) as a profession. Despite her initial skepticism, she fell in love with the field and excelled in it.

These stories highlight the importance of balancing personal interests with parental guidance. While one student followed her passion, the other went with her parents' suggestion, but both ultimately found success. In such a situation, it is essential to recognize one's interests, consider the suggestions of parents or caregivers, seek advice from a career counselor, and then make an informed decision.

In conclusion, convincing parents or getting convinced by them is a critical decision-making process that requires a thoughtful balance of interests, suggestions, and advice. It is ultimately the student's life and career, and they should have the final say in their career path, but it is also vital to listen to the wisdom and guidance of those who care about their well-being

Grown up v/s not so mature:

"You need to grow up", "you are an adult now stop acting like a kid", "don't interfere when adults are talking", "you don't know anything you are just a child"; and all these statements are something any young adult listens to almost every day. One of the confusion that students in their late teens and early twenties face is that whether they are still children or adults. For some things, a 'grown up' tag is attached to them while other time 'still not mature enough' tag is attached. They are adult enough to vote but still a child when it comes to make major decisions of their life? At times they are old enough to start looking after themselves but not so mature enough to go out on trips or even think about studying in different cities?

These contradicting statements that come from the environment they live in, not only weakens their confidence but also stuns their mental growth and create a sense of confusion in them.

It is true there cannot be just black and white in this situation, but it is also important that the grays and the blurred lines don't become the reason of a mental chaos.

Being in controlled environment v/s being self-disciplined:

As they approach adulthood, young people are faced with important decisions about their future. They are expected to make decisions about their education, career, relationships, and more, but they may not feel confident or prepared to do so. The constant messages of "you don't know anything, you're just a child" can undermine their confidence and make them doubt their ability to make good decisions.

Moreover, when they step into the world of college, they are faced with a new environment that is different from the one they grew up in. They are no longer in a controlled environment where everything is filtered and regulated, but instead are faced with a new level of freedom and responsibility. They are expected to manage their own lives, make their own decisions, and deal with the consequences of those decisions.

It is true that this transition can be challenging, but it is also an essential part of growing up. The sudden shift from a protected environment to an unknown and unregulated world can be both exciting and scary. But this change also presents an opportunity for young people to learn self-discipline, decision-making, and character growth.

The key is to find a balance between being self-disciplined and embracing the newfound freedom that comes with adulthood.

While it can be tempting to throw caution to the wind and do whatever feels good in the moment, it is important to recognize that there are consequences to every action. On the other hand, being too strict and regimented can stifle growth and creativity.

The road to adulthood is a journey filled with challenges and obstacles, but it is also a time of great growth and discovery. Young people should take advantage of this time to learn more about themselves and the world around them, and to find the balance that works best for them. It is a time to embrace the opportunities and responsibilities of adulthood, while still holding on to the wonder and curiosity of childhood.

Higher salary v/s 'Brand' Company:

Making a decision between a higher salary or working for a brand company can often leave individuals in a dilemma. The choice is not an easy one to make as both options have their own set of advantages and disadvantages.

Working for a smaller company or startup comes with the benefit of receiving a better pay. A smaller company tends to have fewer employees, which means more hands-on experience and opportunities to work on a wider range of projects. This can result in a more holistic development and learning experience. With less bureaucracy and hierarchy, the smaller company can offer a more personalized and unique work environment. Employees can feel more appreciated and have a chance to work in close collaboration with senior members of the team. However, the downside to working in a small company is the lack of overall exposure to big projects and the inability to tap into a wider audience.

Working for a big brand company can offer a lot of exposure and networking opportunities. A well-established company tends to have a structured workflow, a wider audience, and a more prominent place in the industry. This can provide valuable learning experiences and boost career prospects. However, the downside to working for a big company is the rigidity of the workflow. The company may have specific protocols that must be adhered to, and there may be less room for creativity or exploration. Employees may find themselves limited to a specific role or function, and after a certain point, there may not be much more to learn.

When making the decision, it's essential to weigh the pros and cons of both options. One must consider their career goals, personal development, and future prospects. It's important to choose an option that aligns with one's personal values and interests. If an individual prefers a personalized and unique work environment and enjoys hands-on learning, a smaller company or startup may be the best option. However, if an individual prefers a structured work environment and is seeking to network and gain more exposure in the industry, working for a big brand company may be the way to go. Ultimately, it is essential to prioritize personal growth and job satisfaction over salary or brand value.

Job seeker v/s Job provider:

In the world of employment, the classic dilemma for many is deciding whether to be a job seeker or a job provider. The distinction between the two is quite apparent. Job seekers are individuals who prefer to work for someone else or a company and lead smaller teams for specific projects. They take pride in their work, and as long as they are satisfied with their performance and are part of a team that aligns with their interests, they are content with their position.

On the other hand, job providers, most commonly known as entrepreneurs, have a creative spark within them that drives them to take risks and innovate. They seek autonomy and independence, and the idea of being in control of their work and their team is what motivates them to start their own businesses or ventures. They take on leadership roles and lead teams to work on projects that they are passionate about. They strive to create their own success stories and inspire others to do the same.

Both paths have their unique benefits and drawbacks. Being a job seeker can lead to a more structured work-life with fewer risks, allowing individuals to focus on their work and grow in a well-established company. On the other hand, being a job provider involves taking on more risks but also offers more control over one's work, creativity, and income. It's up to each individual to decide which path aligns with their interests, skills, and goals.

Higher Education v/s Job:

Making a choice between further studies and a job is not easy, especially after reaching certain education milestones such as 10th, 12th, graduation or post-graduation. It can be quite a dilemma for students to decide what to do next. However, there is no one-size-fits-all answer to this question. The right choice depends on each individual's career aspirations, interests and long-term goals.

If someone is keen to learn more and explore the academic field, then going for further studies is the right choice. This decision will not only expand their knowledge and skills but also open up many opportunities for them. By pursuing advanced education, they will gain in-depth knowledge and develop a deeper understanding of their chosen field, which can lead to better job prospects and salary increments.

On the other hand, those who don't wish to study anymore and want to dive into the world of work can opt for a job. For these individuals, practical, on-the-job experience can provide better learning and growth opportunities. Working in their chosen field can help them gain real-world experience, develop important skills and make valuable industry connections. They can learn and grow in their field through practical experience, and with hard work and dedication, they can climb the ladder of success.

In the end, it is important to choose a path that aligns with one's interests, goals and aspirations. Whether it is further studies or a job, the key is to stay focused and committed to achieving success in one's chosen field.

Professional v/s Vocational course

Ah, the age-old dilemma of choosing between a professional education and a vocational course! It's no secret that people often overlook the power of vocational education and blindly run after professions for the sake of monetary gain. But let me tell you, my friend, choosing the right game for you is all about recognizing your strengths and devising a strategy that works best for your playground.

Vocational courses provide you with hands-on training and practical skills that are highly sought-after by employers. They equip you with the necessary knowledge and expertise in a specific field, leading to a fulfilling career and a satisfying life. It's time we stop underestimating the value of vocational education and start seeing it as a game-changer in the career world.

However, it's important to note that there's no right or wrong choice between a professional education and a vocational course. It all comes down to your personal goals, interests, and priorities. What's crucial is that you make an informed decision that aligns with your strengths and your aspirations.

So, my dear friend, don't just blindly run after professions. Instead, choose a game that aligns with your strengths and interests, and strategize accordingly. Remember, success is not just about the money, but about finding personal fulfillment and satisfaction in your career.

Career in Sports?

It's not uncommon for children to have a passion for a certain sport or activity, but due to various reasons, they are forced to give up on it. I had a student, Pratuysh, who was always interested in cricket but lacked the natural talent for it, so his parents steered him towards a Bachelor's degree in Commerce. After just six months in the program, he came to me seeking advice. It turned out that he had a talent for doodling and sketching, and was especially good at live sketching cricket matches. He realized he could connect his passion for cricket with his hobby of sketching, and set out to pursue a career in this innovative field.

Similarly, I also know a mechanical engineer who writes sports blogs simply because of his love for sports. A career in sports doesn't have to be limited to just playing the game. In fact, the world of sports comprises of various professions, such as sports management companies, coaches, commentators, talent finders, sports journalists, sports bloggers, and many more.

Many people have achieved a great level of success in their career through their involvement in sports. However, it's understandable that parents might be hesitant to support their child in pursuing a career in sports, given the perceived uncertainty of this choice. But it's important to remember that there is always a level of uncertainty that exists in every profession. It's worth exploring and discussing the possibilities of a career in sports with your child, as it may open up a world of opportunities that they never thought were possible. The topic of a career in sports is discussed in more detail later in this book.

Career in performing arts?

Step into the captivating world of the performing arts, where the limelight shines bright and the stage is set for endless possibilities. Despite being a field that boasts immense creativity and entertainment value, it's also one that is often perceived as unpredictable and uncertain. Careers in the performing arts can range from musicians, dancers, singers, actors, and beyond - each profession demanding a unique set of skills that are built upon a foundation of raw talent and dedication.

But why is this field considered uncertain, you may ask? Simply put, the value of a performing artist is tied to their ability to produce outstanding art and make a name for themselves in a highly competitive industry. And although the performing arts have gained tremendous popularity, it still remains an unconventional career choice for many.

But don't let the uncertain nature of this field deter you from pursuing your passion. From the iconic masterpieces of Mozart and Picasso to the mesmerizing performances of Beyonce and the timeless contributions of MF Hussain, Amitabh Bachchan, and Pt. Shiv Kumar - each of these legends have left an indelible mark on the world of performing arts.

So why not carve out your own niche in this exciting and dynamic field? Whether you're a singer who can hit those high notes effortlessly, a dancer who moves with grace and fluidity, or an actor who can captivate an audience with every word, the performing arts is a space where talent and hard work can take you to new heights. So take a bow and let your star shine bright!

What if I fail?

Don't be disheartened if you stumble and fall, for failure is not the end of the road, but merely the first step towards success. The fear of failure is a common obstacle that many students grapple with, as they fret over the possibility of making the wrong choices and not reaching their desired career goals. But what if we told you that failure could be the catalyst for something great?

Instead of allowing fear to cripple your ambition, what if you shifted your perspective to one of possibility and potential? What if you dared to dream big and took calculated risks in pursuit of your goals? What if you envisioned success instead of dwelling on the possibility of failure?

It's important to remember that your mind is a powerful tool, capable of shaping your thoughts and actions in ways that can either propel you towards success or hold you back. By cultivating a positive mindset and focusing on the possibilities rather than the pitfalls, you can create a path towards achievement and fulfillment.

So, the next time you encounter a setback or stumble on the road to success, remember that it's not the end of the journey. Rather, it's an opportunity to learn, grow, and improve. Embrace the challenge and stay focused on your goals, for with hard work and determination, the possibility of success is within reach. Let the fear of failure be replaced with the thrill of possibility, and watch as your dreams come to life.

Life is a game of balance, a delicate dance that requires you to strike a harmony between your choices, goals, standards, and values. Each decision you make has the power to influence your future, and so it's crucial that you approach decision-making with care and consideration.

The key to making informed decisions is first and foremost to understand your "SELF"(Discussed in later in the book). You must take the time to reflect on your 5 p's. This process of self-discovery is critical to making decisions that align with your personal and professional aspirations.

Then you have identify your values, and begin to create SMART goals - Specific, Measurable, Achievable, Realistic, and Timely. These goals will provide you with a clear direction and a sense of purpose, helping you to stay focused on your aspirations.

To ensure that your decisions align with your goals and values, it's important to establish a set of standards or principles that you can use to evaluate your options. These standards can serve as a guiding light, helping you to make choices that are consistent with your core beliefs and values.

Remember, making informed decisions is not just about making the right choice, but also about having the confidence to stick with your decision and make it right. Once you have made a decision, it's important to take ownership of it, to take action, and to adapt as necessary.

By using these strategies, you can make decisions that will set you on the path towards personal and professional growth and development, helping you to achieve your long-term career goals and gain a brighter future. So take the time to know yourself, establish your goals and values, and make informed decisions that will pave the way for a fulfilling and rewarding life.

Parent's Dilemma

As a parent, you know that your child is the most important thing in your life. From the moment they enter your world, you become their first teacher, guide, and protector. You create a safe and secure environment for them to grow and thrive, shielding them from the world's harsh realities. But as they grow older, you face countless dilemmas about their future.

One of the biggest dilemmas that parents face is deciding on the right career path for their child. Many parents have an unshakeable preference for certain careers like engineering, medicine, law, and others that offer financial stability, respect in society, and a secure future. They believe that these careers will provide their children with the best possible chances of success and a good life.

However, many parents also fear unconventional career choices as they are often filled with uncertainty. They worry that their child will face a difficult road ahead if they choose a career that is not well-established or has a limited job market. It's a balancing act between allowing your child to pursue their passions and guiding them towards a career that will offer them stability and success.

In addition to career choices, parents face a host of other dilemmas when it comes to their relationship with their child. They may worry about being too overprotective or not protective enough, and they may struggle to find the right balance between supporting and guiding their child and giving them the space to make their own decisions.

Another dilemma parents face is deciding how much influence they should have over their child's choices. They want to guide their child towards making the best decisions, but they also don't want to control their child's life. Finding the right balance can be challenging, but it's essential to give your child the freedom to make their own choices while also offering support and guidance along the way.

Ultimately, as a parent, you want the best for your child, and making decisions about their future can be overwhelming. But by recognizing your own fears and biases, communicating openly with your child, and encouraging them to pursue their passions, you can help guide them towards a fulfilling and successful life. Your child's life is their own, and it's up to them to choose their own path. As a parent, your role is to support and guide them towards making the best decisions for themselves.

Friendly parents v/s friend parents

Which one is better? Parents those are friendly? Or parents who are like friends? Parents try hard to understand their kids so that they can form a connection and improve their relationship. But they get stuck in the in the dilemma of where to put a line. Being a friendly parent means having an open mind and to be understanding towards your child. A friend like parent is also kind of similar except the fact that there might be a more frank relationship between the parent and the child. Having a friendly aspect in a parent-child relationship can prove to be beneficial if a proper balance with respect and communication is shaped.

Coaching class v/s Self-study:

Another dilemma that parents these days face is that of whether they should provide their child with coaching classes or let him/her study on their own. There are some students who study better in a group and some study better when alone, It is essential for parents to observe and find out what works better for their child. Coaching centers or classes can help a child to understand the basic concept but it is the hard work and self-study that matters the most. So, if required the parents should provide coaching classes to their children but that does not mean there is no need for self-study. I always propagated self-study as best study

Co-curriculum v/s academics:

Many preach the importance of a balance between the academics and co-curricular activities in a student's life. But as the student reaches high-school most parents and teachers ask students to just focus on their studies and drop any form of sport or art they are involved in. This suggestion comes from the idea that anything other than studies will be distracting for their child. Do you agree with this? Well, let me tell you about Sameer, a very talented volleyball player. Sameer was extremely talented in his sports but not so much in academics, his parents like most parents were worried about his future. During the last fewmonths of his 12th grade and just before the exams he went for national volleyball matches even though his parents and teachers were reluctant about it. Sameer went to one of the well-known college in the Capital even though his percentage wasn't that good. How? Because of his participation in the national level match. Though he scored below average, he was in the same prestigious course and college as the topper of his class. In Sameer's case his talent and dedication towards volleyball bared him same fruits as topper.

Academics and co-curriculums should be given equal importance. Not every student is good in studies; some have talent in other fields which should be given equal amount of importance.

Child's interest v/s child's career:

Another dilemma for parents is when it comes to child's interest v/s child's career. When a child shows interest in an unconventional career choice the major worry of parents is, how will he/she form a career of this? Is there even a career in this field? This sometimes leads to parents forcing their conventional career choices on their children.

Four years ago, a family friend told me about her son, who was at this moment in 12th grade and was doing well in studies. What worried his mother was that even though he was showed interest in many things, he never stuck with anything more than six months. Recently I got to hear that the very same child was now practicing to become a pandit and is even looking forward to study for the Acharya level. I was quite shocked to learn this development, how did a child who used to run away when told to study was not learning long Sanskrit mantras on his own? The answer I got to know was simple. The mother never forced her to any career and let her son find himself whatever profession he was interested in.

These days young adults are focusing more on what brings them satisfaction even if it's unconventional. Parents should understand that a child's happiness matters more.

Chapter 2

TURACHE? TURACHE!!!

As a child, there was one word that I heard repeatedly and that shaped me in a profound way: "turache." My father would often use this word whenever I spoke about other people or their actions. He would ask me, "Turache?" which essentially meant, "But what about yourself?" This simple yet powerful question motivated me to reflect on my own thoughts and actions, and ultimately helped me to become more self-aware and mindful.

I believe that this concept of turache is something that everyone should know and understand, as it can have a transformative effect on our lives. But where did this word come from, and what is its significance?

The story behind turache begins with a king named Darius, the ruler of the Persian Empire. They were very proud of themselves. He had inherited a great army and an even greater kingdom from his forefathers and was full of himself about all the wealth and prosperity that surrounded him.

Adding to his pride, there were people in his court who kept him in this false impression of his greatness. The high priest of the temple kept boasting about the unconditional grace of their god, The Lord of the Celestial Flame, Ahura Mazda. The head of the cavalry was more than confident about the opulence of their soldiers.

Darius was only a personification of glory of his kingdom and the forefathers and only kept working on their thoughts. He had never taken the trouble to search for his views or make his personality. He was neither a warrior nor a king. His exalted majesty was made up of the soldier's actions and the intelligence of the officials in his court. He had never faced a situation in which he would take any responsibility.

His army was so massive that any army which dared to challenge was frightened and awed by the pomp and show of vast and disciplined army with their Silver Blades and Golden armor. The secret for the expansion and strength of the Persian Empire was the grandeur of the great Persian army, and the king never played any significant role in it.

But the king himself was unsure of the longevity of the empire and his reign as he lacked self-reliance under cover of pride. In these times, the Persian Empire was challenged by a Greek who was a renowned hero of the times and was known for the warrior ship and battle skills and was said to be charging from the west like a hurricane. The armies were to face off in the place called Gaugamela. The Persian army was as always ready in the field in its grand form. But Darius was somehow nervous and was meddling in his mind with the thoughts of his father.

Finally, the Greek army arrived, and they looked like a bunch of undisciplined soldiers in Iron and Bronze. The leader came directly to see Darius. He removed his Bronze helm with an Ostrich feather, and there was this light in his eyes, which expressed self-reliance a lot more than confidence. It was a massive ocean of the power which he carried in his self and Darius was shaken by the persona of this Greek boy.

The custom was that the king's translator would start the conversation by introducing the king, but Darius became so restless that he stood up and word came flowing out of his mouth "Pidram Sultan bood" (my forefathers were great kings). Nobody had any idea why was the king of the great Persian empire behaving like that in front of a Greek boy with a bunch of soldiers. But it wasn't the army or the strength, but the flare in the eyes that had shaken the king. The Greek boy, by the name of Alexander has remained irritatingly calm, which disturbed Darius. With the great calmness and a smile on his face, he spoke with confidence, in Persian "Turache?" This act of courage was enough, for the spirit, Darius had been faking, and it went down crumbling. Eyes and confidence in Alexander's personality had already shaken; the king and this simple question in his language by a Greek boy had made him shudder from the inside. Again a thought of his father swept across his mind "A king must have a last word." Then he shook this thought away, "Oh! Let me be now Pader(father)......"

The translator then began, "There stands before you O! Lord Darius the Emperor of the Great Persia...." But the effect was already made, the battle already won. After the meeting was dispersed and throughout the day, Darius was enthralled to think of only those words, "Turache? Turache?", which meant "Who are you?"In the dark of the night, he went out of his camp thinking about what he was other than heir to a well-established and running empire what was his actual self and thinking this he kept walking and never came back.

When I first heard this story the first thought that came in my mind was the king of a vast empire was also made to think about his actual self and compelled to give up since he had nothing of his own and nothing in his personality. And Alexander was renowned as Alexander, The Great because of the great personality he carried and the self-confidence that he was full of, which led to the opening of the gate of the eastern continents an Asia to the western powers which was till then blocked by the Great Persian empire for centuries.

The question "Turache?" is not just a simple phrase, but it holds a significant power in helping us shift our perspective and become more self-aware. By asking ourselves this question, we are forced to take a step back and reflect on our own thoughts and actions. It reminds us to take responsibility for our own growth and development, and strive to become the best version of ourselves.

The power of Turache lies in its ability to guide us towards understanding our true selves. It encourages us to explore our passions, potential and personality. Through this exploration, we gain insight into who we are, and how we can develop ourselves to become the person we want to be.

We learn from the story above that no matter what we face, we can achieve great feats with the right attitude and a strong personality. However, developing these traits is not a one-time effort. It requires continuous effort and a commitment to our personal growth.

The journey towards self-discovery is essential as it helps us understand our foundation, our character, our dreams and our capabilities. It gives us a deeper understanding of our purpose in life, which is like a guiding light that leads us towards fulfilling our potential.

As we embark on this journey, we start building our character, understanding our self-worth and boosting our self-confidence. We start to see ourselves in a new light, with a clearer understanding of who we are and what we want from life.

Through this process of self-discovery, we become better individuals and thus benefit society as a whole. We become more compassionate, empathetic and understanding of others. We become agents of positive change, inspiring others to embark on their own journey of self-discovery.

To embark on a journey of self-discovery, it is important to start by reflecting on the meaning and purpose we give to our lives. This is the foundation for our personal growth and development. By embracing the power of introspection and reflection, we can take the first step towards uncovering our true selves and unlocking our full potential. Let us embrace this process of self-discovery and see where it leads us.

Chapter 3

DISCOVER YOUR "*SELF*"

Do I have a story for you! It's a story about my own discovery of *SELF*, and how a single question helped me realize my true calling in life. It all started when I was growing up in an environment where science was considered to be the most important field, and a government job was seen as the only way to be successful. Unfortunately, I ended up internalizing this belief as well, which limited my perspective for a long time.

After finishing my graduation, I tried to clear many government exams but failed every time. As you can imagine, it was a pretty tough time for me. But then, something unexpected happened. I started giving tuition classes like any other child my age. And to my surprise, I discovered that I had a natural talent for teaching. Before I knew it, my tuition classes were growing at a rapid pace, with so many students that two floors of my home were not enough, and some students even had to sit on the stairs!

Despite the success of my tuition classes, I still felt like a failure because I was "unemployed." I didn't have a brand name behind me, and my success was only recognized by my own name or the name I gave to my classes. So when a job opportunity finally came my way, I took it without thinking twice. Although the pay was much less than what I was earning from my tuition classes, having a job gave me a sense of satisfaction of being employed at the time.

But soon enough, I realized that the job wasn't really me, and I left it. I was still feeling lost and unsure of what to do next. It was only when someone asked me about my job profile, and I told them about my tuition classes and self-employment, that they gave me a new perspective. They replied, "Oh! So you're an entrepreneur?" It was a moment of realization for me, and it gave me many questions to ponder upon, like what is entrepreneurship, can tuitions be regarded as employment, and how can I grow my business? Most importantly, I started to ask myself why I was taking classes in the first place and what meaning I wanted to give to my life.

I soon discovered the concept of "Meaning Making," which is about identifying our values, passions, and purpose, and creating meaning in our lives. By embracing this concept, I was able to recognize my true potential and pursue my passion for teaching. I also realized that I was never a failure because I wasn't running a race to be successful; I was on my journey to something that made meaning for me.

So, if you're feeling lost or confused about your path in life, try to embrace the concept of "Meaning Making." Identify your 'SELF', know your why and allow it to guide you towards your true calling. You never know, you might just have your own 'eureka' moment, and find your own unique path to success and fulfilment.

Meaning Making

To make the most out of your quest for purpose and meaning, it's time to move away from the outdated practice of relying on checklists to determine students' traits and presenting them with a limited pool of job options. The world is constantly evolving, and the way we approach choosing careers has to change with it, particularly during the crucial transition period from high school to university or the working world.

During this critical period, students are not only seeking to gain a deep understanding of the content they're studying, but also searching for greater meaning and purpose. As educators, we can guide them by encouraging them to engage in contemplative practices such as discussions, research, analysis, evaluation, and synthesis of key concepts.

The key to making meaning is to offer students the freedom to demonstrate their comprehension of the content in a way that is personalized to their unique strengths and interests. This means encouraging them to try new things, explore their passions, and discover their skills. The more they experiment, the more likely they are to find what truly resonates with them. Once they've found their passion and purpose, they can focus on that area as a potential career choice.

Consider the case of Shivi, who discovered his natural inclination towards the mechanical workings of machines early on when he created a robot soccer player in seventh grade. Despite this, he was pressured into pursuing computer science engineering in college. However, he struggled and realized that he needed to pursue his true calling. He eventually started his own music company, but it wasn't fulfilling his quest for purpose and meaning.

With our guidance, Shivi restarted his career in the field of machine learning, using his skills to help young people pursue their passions. This case study highlights the fact that the possibilities in every field are endless, but it's up to each individual to identify their area of interest and pursue it wholeheartedly. By embracing our unique strengths and passions, we can truly flourish and find meaning in our journey

As a student, **embarking on your quest for a meaningful life** requires knowing five critical elements. Let's delve deeper into each of these aspects to help you navigate this journey successfully.

Firstly, you must **know your why**. Why are you studying what you are studying, and what is your ultimate goal? Understanding the purpose behind your actions will provide you with the necessary motivation to achieve your objectives. For example, a student who is pursuing medicine must ask themselves, "Why do I want to become a doctor?" Is it to save lives, to bring relief to people who are suffering, or to make a difference in the world? Knowing your why will give you direction and purpose.

Secondly**, know your inclinations**. What are your interests, passions, and natural talents? It's crucial to recognize your unique abilities and lean towards your natural inclinations when choosing a career path. For instance, if you enjoy working with your hands and have a fascination for design, architecture might be a good fit for you.

Thirdly, **define what success means to you**. Success is not a one-size-fits-all definition, and everyone has their unique definition of what it means to be successful. Some people equate success with wealth and fame, while others believe it's about making a difference in the world. It's crucial to determine what success looks like for you so that you can work towards achieving it. For example, a student who defines success as being able to provide medical assistance to people in underprivileged areas might aim to become a doctor who volunteers their services in such regions.

Fourthly, **identify the subjects that interest you the most**. These are the subjects that ignite your passion and inspire you to learn more. When you enjoy what you're studying, it's easier to stay motivated and invested in your learning. For instance, a student who loves history might decide to pursue a career in archaeology or become a historian.

Lastly, **identify who your ideal person is**. Who is the role model that you look up to and aspire to be like? It could be a famous celebrity, a family member, or even a teacher. Understanding who you want to model your life after can provide you with a clear direction of what you want to achieve. For example, a student who admires Elon Musk might decide to pursue a career in technology and innovation.

In conclusion, knowing these five critical elements is essential to finding meaning in your quest for a fulfilling life. By understanding your why, inclinations, definition of success, favorite subjects, and role model, you can create a roadmap that leads to a successful and fulfilling life. Remember, this is a journey unique to each individual, so take the time to reflect, explore and discover what makes you happy and fulfilled.

Let me share with you an inspiring case study of one of my students named Nona, who discovered her true passion and found success by following the 5 key elements to making meaning in her life.

Nona was an exceptional student, brilliant and charismatic, who excelled in school and college with outstanding grades. Despite being encouraged to pursue the conventional path of science, which is traditionally considered the top choice for high achievers like herself, Nona never truly identified with the academic subject. She was accepted into one of the most prestigious private colleges on a full scholarship, but even there, she felt like something was missing.

Despite her high grades, Nona's true passion was dance. She pursued it with equal dedication and even joined a reputed dance organization. However, she eventually realized that her true calling was not in that field either. With guidance, she decided to complete her degree while pursuing her interest in dance as a hobby or extracurricular activity.

Nona joined the university dance society and helped the team earn many accolades in competitions. As she explored and tried new things, she discovered that what she really wanted was to become a celebrity in the entertainment industry for her acting and dancing skills.

With the help of her parents, Nona decided to follow her dreams and pursue her definition of success. She worked hard and today, she is carrying on with her life just how she always wanted, with contentment and without any second thoughts.

Nona's case study illustrates the importance of the 5 key elements to making meaning in one's life. First, knowing your "why" or your purpose in life. Second, knowing your inclinations and what sparks your passion. Third, defining your own version of success. Fourth, identifying which subjects you enjoy the most. And finally, finding an ideal or role model to look up to.

Despite being an outstanding student with high grades in all subjects, Nona realized that academic excellence alone wasn't enough to find fulfillment and meaning in life. She had to explore and try new things, and follow her true passion and calling to be truly happy and content.

Her story is a testament to the fact that success is not just about following the traditional path of high profile corporate jobs, but rather it is about finding your own unique path and pursuing what truly brings you joy and fulfillment.

When we talk about meaning-making, we're speaking about sustainable career options that explain the ever-changing dynamic world. Technology is advancing at such a rapid pace that it's accelerated the scale, nature, dynamics, and speed of information, knowledge, concepts, and applications. This change no longer allows us to stick to one job or career, but instead, we need effective options that can give our lives meaning. Hence, it becomes crucial for us to recognize what we should do and what we should opt for in our professional lives.

From the very beginning, the desire to be a leader in my life motivated me. I was attracted to anything and everything that came my way, and I explored various fields. But it was then that I realized I was keen on socio-intellectual leadership and not political or business leadership. For me, it became a concept of the teaching of maths or maths of teaching.

While teaching many students, I came across Puru, a very ambitious boy who was outstanding in academics but had a keen interest in cricket. For him, it was challenging to choose between cricket or something related to academics. When he came to me for a suggestion, I asked him to stand in front of the mirror and reflect on his five critical elements: Why he wants what he wants, what his inclinations are, what success means for him, the subject he resonates most with, and his role model. It was then that he realized he sees himself as a successful sportsman and went on to pursue his interest in cricket.

Despite the fact that many parents today don't allow their kids to go for anything extra apart from the school curriculum, I had a student who was very courageous in following his interest in the arts. I can still feel the spark in his eyes when he said that he would soon invite me as a guest in his exhibition.

In a world that's constantly evolving, meaning-making has become more critical than ever. It's not just about finding a job that pays the bills, but finding something that truly resonates with you. Understanding your five critical elements is a crucial part of that process. It can help you identify your passions, your goals, and ultimately, lead you towards a career that provides a sense of purpose and fulfillment.

Identify Your '*SELF*'

By understanding your Five Critical Elements Why, Inclinations, Meaning of success, Subject of Interest, and role model. you can make decisions that truly resonate with who you are and what you want out of life. In fact, this approach works well for around 68.2% of people.

However, for some folks, it's not so simple. They struggle to differentiate between their genuine feelings and what they think they should be feeling. This can make it challenging to make decisions that feel authentic and aligned with their innermost desires.

For example, let's say you're trying to choose a career path. The Five Critical Elements suggest that you should consider your Why, Inclinations, Meaning of success, Subject of Interest, and role model to find a path that suits you. But if you're someone who has trouble separating your own desires from external influences (like societal expectations or family pressure), you might feel stuck.

If this sounds like you, don't worry! There are some things you can do to connect with your true self and make decisions that feel right. Here are 5 Ps to Identify your *SELF*.

Have you ever gazed at the bright beam of light emanating from a lighthouse, guiding ships through the tumultuous sea? In much the same way, our purpose serves as a beacon, illuminating the path we must take to fulfill our potential and achieve our aspirations. Our purpose defines the broader direction we need to move in, providing clarity and focus. For some, like myself, that direction may lie in the realm of education, but each individual's purpose is unique and deeply personal.

Discovering our purpose is not a simple formula or equation. It requires introspection, and a deep understanding of our passions, potential, and personality. Additionally, the influence of our parents and the environment we grow up in can shape and mold our purpose, sometimes altering the course of our lives entirely.

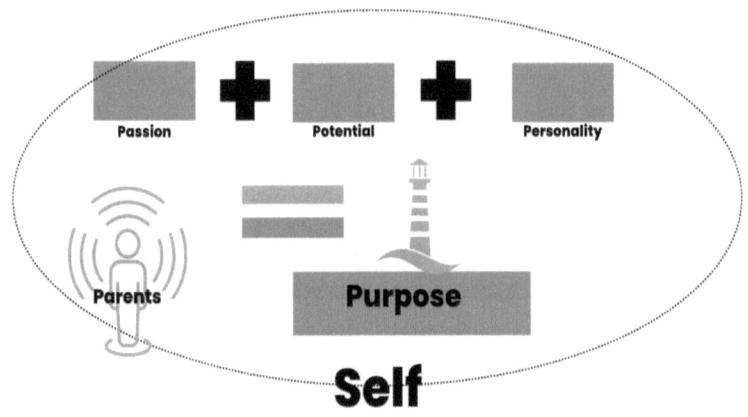

The "*Self*" is comprised of all five elements - passion, potential, personality, parents, and purpose. Each of these components is essential to the rare and precious entity that is the "Self". Without any one of these elements, the true essence of the "Self" is lost.

By seeking to understand and honor our purpose, we can unlock the full potential of our "*Self*". With each step we take towards our purpose, we grow and develop, becoming ever more capable and fulfilled. So let us strive to discover and pursue our purpose, and in doing so, unlock the full potential of our "*Self*" and live our most authentic and fulfilling lives. The concept of meaning-making has become essential in today's world. It involves finding the right balance between the 5Ps to achieve the best outcome for a child. All of these five components play an important role in a child's life, especially when they're searching for their true identity. However, it's essential to understand that every child has a unique formula for meaning-making, and not every child can achieve the perfect balance of all five components.

During my years of career coaching, I've observed that many students are confused and unaware of their true "*Self*." They aren't sure what they like, and many aren't even sure of their aim. It's a sad reality that most students are so caught up in the rat race of life that they forget who they truly are. But with the 5Ps of *SELF*, we can help them discover their passion, potential, purpose, personality, and the role of their parents in guiding them towards their true selves.

So, the question remains, do you know who you are? What is your passion, and where does your potential lie? With the 5Ps of *SELF*, we can bridge the gap between our passions and potentials and help us find our purpose in life. Just like the four-leaf clover, our true "*Self*" is unique and rare, and with the 5Ps of *SELF*, we can nurture and cherish it to its fullest potential.

Passion

Have you ever woken up at the crack of dawn, with an insatiable drive to tackle the day ahead? Or have you found yourself completely immersed in a task, losing track of time and feeling completely invigorated after hours of hard work? These moments can feel like magic, but they are actually a result of something very real and very powerful: passion.

Passion is that spark that ignites your soul and fuels your energy, pushing you to pursue something with enthusiasm and dedication. It brings a sense of meaning and purpose to your life, and when you find it, you know you've struck gold.

But how do you uncover your passion? It's a question that has puzzled many of us, but the answer lies within yourself. Start by exploring your interests and what makes you truly happy. Think about the activities that light you up inside, and the subjects you love learning about. Reflect on your natural skills and talents, and the things you excel at effortlessly. These clues can lead you in the direction of your passion.

If you're still struggling to identify your passion, don't worry - you're not alone. You can ask yourself some pointed questions to help you uncover it. What subjects fascinate you? What careers have you considered in the past? What do you find yourself naturally drawn to, even in your free time? If money were no object, what would you do?

It's also important to try new things and expand your horizons. Attend events and join clubs that relate to your interests, take classes or courses to learn more about a subject that intrigues you, and allow yourself to be open to new experiences. You never know - your passion may be waiting for you in a place you never would have thought to look.

Remember, it may take time and effort to discover your passion, but it's worth the journey. When you do find it, it can lead to a life full of fulfillment and purpose. So keep searching and exploring, and don't give up until you find that spark that ignites your soul.

Now let's do a quick exercise that might help you identify your passion:

Look at the list and realise the core passion.
"What makes you feel full of life??"

___ Accomplishment ___ Accumulation ___ Achievement ___ Activity ___ Actualization ___ Adventure ___ Altruism ___ Art ___ Authenticity ___ Awareness ___ Awe ___ Balance ___ Beauty ___ Being ___ Bonding ___ Challenge ___ Change ___ Clarity ___ Communication ___ Compassion ___ Competency ___ Connection ___ Consciousness ___ Construction ___ Creativity ___ Curiosity ___ Deep Feelings ___ Development ___ Discovery ___ Education ___ Empowerment ___ Enlightenment ___ Enterprise ___ Environment ___ Equality ___ Examination ___ Excitement ___ Expansion ___ Exploration ___ Expression ___ Fairness ___ Fitness ___ Flow

___ Freedom ___ Fulfillment ___ Fun ___ Godliness ___ Goodness ___ Happiness ___ Healing ___ Helping ___ Humor ___ Imagination ___ Improvement ___ Ingenuity ___ Innovation ___ Insight ___ Inspiration ___ Intimacy ___ Joy ___ Justice ___ Knowledge ___ Leadership ___ Learning ___ Leisure ___ Logic ___ Love ___ Lucidity ___ Making a Difference ___ Meaning ___ Meaningful Experiences ___ Money ___ Music ___ Nature ___ Nurture ___ Opportunity ___ Origination ___ Patriotism ___ Peace ___ Personal Growth ___ Play ___ Power ___ Precision ___ Problem-Solving

___ Purpose ___ Realization ___ Relationships ___ Relaxation ___ Restoration ___ Romance ___ Self-Expression ___ Selflessness ___ Serenity ___ Serving ___ Sharing ___ Socializing ___ Spirituality ___ Status ___ Strength ___ Success ___ Synergy ___ Teaching ___ Teamwork ___ Tradition ___ Tranquility ___ Travel ___ Truth ___ Understanding ___ Unity ___ Usefulness ___ Visualization ___ Vitality ___ Volunteering ___ Winning ___ Working ___ Writing

___ Hobby:_____   ___ Subject:_____
___ Sport:_____   ___ The Arts:_____
___ People:_____   ___ Place:_____
___ Thing:_____   ___ _____

https://www.sterling.edu/sites/default/files/Passion%20Discovery%20Worksheet.pdf

Potential

Passion and potential are like bread and butter; they go together. While having passion is great, it's not enough if it doesn't align with our potential. This is why it's important to bridge our passion with our potential, as it allows us to achieve satisfaction and efficiency.

For instance, let me tell you a story about my student Pyu. He was not the best academically, but he had a passion for cricket. Unfortunately, he was an average player, and his parents were worried about his future. However, Pyu had another talent: drawing and sketching. He was really good at it, and his sketchbooks were filled with fantastic artwork. With some guidance, he combined his passion for cricket with his talent for drawing and sketching. He started sketching live cricket matches, capturing the players and the game. This allowed him to pursue his passion for cricket while also using his potential for drawing and sketching.

Let's do a quick exercise. Answer the following question:

- What have been you major achievements?
- Have you ever been awarded for something?
- What problems do your friends tends to share with you most?
- According to your teachers, what are you best at?
- What is that something your family seek your help for?
- What is that thing you take responsibility for without thinking twice?
- What do you think you are best at?

Welcome to the world of endless possibilities, where potential is our playground, and we get to be the best version of ourselves. It's amazing how much we can achieve when we tap into our full potential. But here's the thing - we need to work on it to unleash its full power. To identify our true potential, we must first recognize what comes naturally to us. Whether it's a creative pursuit or a conventional one, there's something that we excel at without even trying. It's the thing that makes us come alive and feel like we're in our element.

And the best part is, unlocking our potential is not a solo journey. Sometimes, all we need is a coach or guide to help us recognize our true potential at the right moment. With the right support, we can transform our natural talents and skills into something truly exceptional. So, let's embrace our potential, and explore the amazing things we can achieve when we put our minds to it!

https://www.mindtools.com/courses/pdm/funnel1/Explore_Your_Potential.pdf

Personality

Have you ever wondered why some people seem to effortlessly succeed in life, while others struggle to find their footing? Well, it turns out that your personality plays a significant role in shaping your future decisions and outcomes. Some children are driven by their passion, some by their potential, but there are also those whose personalities drive them forward.

Let me share with you the story of one of my students, Shubhu. He was an excellent student with a sharp mind, among the best in his peers academically and otherwise. But what made Shubhu unique was his personality. He was always well-groomed, took initiative in cultural activities, and was attracted to the limelight. After finishing his 12th grade, rather than going to a central university known for its academics, Shubhu chose a private university with a name and status. He pursued a Bachelor's in

Financial Investment and Analysis and even got the opportunity to study in a European country for six months. Shubhu's decision was influenced by all the 5 P's: passion, power, potential, purpose, and personality. He had a passion for managing things, desired power, and had an inclination towards glamour - all a result of his always-on-the-toes personality.

But how do we know if our decisions are influenced by our personality? While it's difficult to categorize individuals into inflexible classes, it can be useful to identify general patterns in our character. Knowing our personality type can provide valuable information about what motivates us and when we are most productive. We can learn a lot about our personality through self-reflection, personality tests, and understanding different character traits.

Realizing our personality type can transform us in many ways, including finding our place and what we need to do to be successful in academics, relationships, finances, and life. Understanding our personality type and that of those around us can help us build better relationships and achieve what we want in life.

If you've been struggling to succeed, it may be because you've been setting the wrong targets for yourself. Taking a personality test can help you unlock your strengths and weaknesses and figure out how to leverage them to achieve your goals. It can also help you identify what you like doing and what you don't like, which can lead to better relationships and a more fulfilling social life.

Having a great personality can help you advance in your career, social, and love life. Employers want to hire people with good people skills, and a good personality can help you get in your boss's good graces. Moreover, if you have a good personality, people will want to spend time with you, opening more doors than you could if your personality wasn't great.

Know your Personality

Did you know that understanding your personality can not only help you improve yourself but also lead you to the perfect career path? It's true! Just like how King Darius was defeated due to his lack of confidence and personality, having a strong sense of self can make all the difference in achieving success.

Your personality is made up of a variety of traits, including your thoughts, attitude, confidence, and strength of character. By recognizing and embracing these traits, you can acquire new skills, decrease stress, and improve your overall lifestyle. But how can you discover your personality type and use it to your advantage?

John Holland's theory of personality offers a useful framework for identifying your strengths and interests. Based on six broad categories, including Realistic, Investigative, Artistic, Social, Enterprising, and Conventional, this theory matches personality traits with suggested career paths. For example, if you have a practical and task-oriented outlook, you might be best suited for a career in engineering, the military, or as an electrician. On the other hand, if you're introspective and enjoy solving complex problems, a career as a systems analyst, chemist, or biologist might be more fulfilling for you.

Imagine for a moment that people were like different pieces in a jigsaw puzzle, each unique in its own way, yet essential to completing the picture. Now, let's take a closer look at some of the pieces that make up this puzzle according to Holland theory

First, we have the "Do-ers." These are the people who thrive on working with their hands and feel most at home around machines, tools, plants, and animals. Their practical, realistic outlook on life makes them great problem solvers, but they prefer to work independently rather than in a team. If you need an electrician, engineer, veterinarian, or someone in the military, these are the folks to call.

Next up, we have the "Thinkers." These are the people who are at their best when they're thinking hard about complex problems. They're analytical, observant, and focused, and they love using logic to come up with creative solutions. They're not so great at persuading others, but that's okay because they prefer to work on their own. If you need a medical technologist, biologist, chemist, or systems analyst, these are the folks to call.

Then we have the "Creators." These are the people who thrive on creativity and expression. They're flexible, impulsive, and emotional, and they love communicating in unique and expressive ways. They value aesthetics highly and enjoy working with designs, patterns, and forms. If you need a musician, reporter, or interior decorator, these are the folks to call.

The "Helpers" are the ones who find joy in teamwork and collaboration. They love solving problems through discussion and providing training or services to others. They're caring, cheerful, and responsible, with a focus on human relationships. If you need a teacher, counselor, or social worker, these are the folks to call.

For the "Persuaders," it's all about taking charge and making things happen. They enjoy persuading others and seek leadership roles. They're assertive, confident, and dominant, and prefer a work environment that allows them to engage in activities that involve leadership, management, and selling. If you need a salesperson, business executive, or manager, these are the folks to call.

Last but not least, we have the "Organizers." These are the people who prefer to work within an established structure and thrive on keeping things organized and running smoothly. They're conscientious, careful, and effective, and they're great at manipulating data, organizing schedules, and operating office equipment. If you need a secretary, accountant, or banker, these are the folks to call.

So, there you have it - the different personalities that make up the puzzle of humanity. Each piece is unique and important, and together they create a beautiful and complex picture.

So, what's your personality type? By understanding your personality and using it to guide your career path, you can unlock your full potential and find success in whatever you choose to pursue.

(https://www.careerkey.org/fit/personality/holland-personality-types#:~:text=According%20to%20John%20Holland's%20theory,Social%2C%20 Enterprising%2C%20and%20Conventional.)

Parents

Our surroundings, our eco-system, and the way we are brought up, are all parts of what make us who we are. Parents play a significant role in shaping our personalities and values, and they are a crucial socio-economic and cultural aspect of our lives. It is a well-known fact that money cannot buy success, but unfortunately, not all children have the same opportunities in life. Unequal distribution of income means that some children have to work harder to achieve their goals.

Adolescents from less privileged backgrounds often mature earlier than their peers, as they have to learn to navigate financial barriers and responsibilities at a young age. In the race to provide their children with the best education, parents often make sacrifices and teach their children to make the most of limited resources. While this can make children more mature and responsible, it can also limit their ability to spread their wings and follow their dreams.

Children from less privileged backgrounds may want to pursue higher education, but they often have to compromise due to limited resources. They may have to choose a career that provides stability and financial security over one that fulfills their passion. It is common to hear children complaining that their parents don't understand them, but the truth is that parents know their children well. They want the best for their kids, but they are often misguided by peer pressure or their own unfulfilled dreams.

Parents who are informed and aware of their children's aspirations and potential play a crucial role in helping them achieve their goals. They provide direction and support, and they encourage their children to pursue what they are passionate about. When children are empowered to pursue their dreams, they are more likely to succeed.

Parents are the primary educators for their children, and they influence their emotional development and personality. When children make wrong decisions or face difficulties, parents are there to guide them and help them make the right choices. They encourage their children to work hard and strive for excellence.

The role of parents is changing with time. They are no longer limited to a few career choices, but have a wide range of options to encourage their children to pursue. Parents can be influencers, but they can also be supporters, guiding their children in their future endeavours.

In conclusion, parents play a significant role in shaping their children's personalities and values. While the financial barriers may be a hindrance to some, supportive and informed parents can empower their children to achieve their dreams. Parents have a crucial role to play in helping their children make the right decisions and work hard to achieve their goals.

Purpose

Have you heard of the captivating tale of Gautama Buddha, the founder of Buddhism? He was born into the illustrious Shakya clan, destined to become a universal monarch or a Buddha. His father sheltered him from the knowledge of religion, human hardship, and the outside world, raising him in a cocoon of comfort after his mother's untimely death. One fateful day, Siddhartha wandered outside his palace and was confronted with the harsh realities of life - old age, disease, death, and suffering. This jarring experience led him to question the meaning of life and the reasons behind human suffering. At the age of 29, he left behind his wife and child to embark on a spiritual journey, filled with years of learning, meditation, and adversity, ultimately leading him to enlightenment and becoming Gautama Buddha. The major turning point in his life was finding his purpose, the reason for his existence.

Now, let's delve into the topic of purpose. Have you ever pondered the questions - what is my purpose? Why do I exist? How should I spend my time? What do I truly desire? How can I achieve it? These questions initiate the process of finding the purpose that gives meaning to our lives. This process is crucial, as it helps us recognize our ultimate aim, the key to our happiness and contentment. It may seem unattainable, but it's always worth pursuing.

By giving purpose to our lives, we come closer to our "Self," gaining a clearer understanding of our desires and goals, which ultimately helps us recognize our purpose. It's like giving direction to an aimless wanderer. Purpose is fueled by a common desire, the yearning for satisfaction. For everyone, satisfaction comes from different aspects of life, making it crucial to understand what defines our happiness to learn more about ourselves.

Let's take three leaders from different professions - an entrepreneur, a politician, and a philanthropist. All three are leaders in their fields, yet their goals and sources of happiness are entirely different. The entrepreneur may strive for better turnover or profit, a more efficient workforce, and a better brand value for the company. The politician's goals may revolve around creating a better impression on society, holistic growth and development of the nation, and winning elections. The philanthropist seeks happiness by helping the less privileged, providing basic needs like education, food, and shelter, increasing awareness at a national or global level, and seeking universal betterment of society.

The difference in the purpose they give to their lives affects every aspect of their existence, from personal to professional lives, even their sense of happiness. Finding purpose in life can help us make better decisions and provide us with a sense of direction. Understanding our purpose can guide our decisions in education, personal life, and career, making our journey more fulfilling.

Take some time to ponder over the questions mentioned above, and find the meaning that you give to your life. Remember, the journey of finding your purpose is what makes it fulfilling. Your purpose is your why, the reason behind all your actions, the foundation of all your decisions. So, enjoy every step of the way!

Chapter 4

FIND YOUR TRUE NORTH

Congratulations on reaching a level of deep self-awareness! By understanding your "*Self*," you have taken a significant step towards realizing your true potential. Now, in order to create a roadmap for your career, a technique called "reverse engineering" is suggested.

What does reverse engineering mean? It simply means starting with Your Purpose in mind and working backward to create a plan to achieve it. In this case, the first step is to identify your purpose. This is the ultimate goal that you want to achieve in your career.

Have you ever heard of the saying, "What you value determines your destiny"? This statement holds true for most people. Just like King Darius, who was defeated because he lacked strong values and beliefs, it is important to establish that your purpose should align with your values. But what exactly are values and how do we identify them?

Values are the things that determine what is important in a person's life and are their priorities. They are a part of a person's identity and influence their behavior, decisions, and personality. When circumstances in one's life align with their values, they feel satisfied and happy, whereas if they go against their values, negative emotions flood their consciousness and affect their mental, emotional, and physical state.

Therefore, discovering your personal core values is crucial to leading a fulfilling and satisfying life. The best way to identify your values is to observe and find what makes you feel good. You can ask yourself questions like, "When did I feel the happiest? What factors contributed to my happiness?" or "When was the time I felt proud? What factors contributed to my feeling of pride?" Once you have identified your top values, prioritize them and reaffirm them.

Knowing your values can also make decision-making and career planning easier. For example, take the case of Romya and Saachi, two friends who completed their schooling together. Romya chose to pursue a Bachelor's in Business Administration because her father was an entrepreneur, while Saachi opted to study for government job exams as both her parents were government officials. Both girls made their choices based on their values or at least what they identified the most with.

However, some children do not have the freedom to make their own choices, and are influenced by family bias. It is essential that a child receives an unbiased environment in order to know their true potential and make their own choices based on their values.

In life, it's important to have a clear purpose and values to guide you towards success and fulfillment. Nelson Mandela, a true inspiration to many, dedicated his life to uplifting others and fought for equality for all. His values were centered around treating everyone equally and providing better education and freedom in his homeland.

Similarly, understanding your own values and priorities can help you make important decisions and create a roadmap to achieve your goals. By identifying your personal core values, you can gain a clear understanding of what truly matters to you and what you stand for. This allows you to make informed decisions that align with your values and helps you stay true to yourself.

Just like Mandela, who stayed committed to his values even during times of adversity, having a strong sense of personal values can help you stay grounded and focused on your goals. It provides you with a personal code of conduct and helps you navigate through life's challenges with clarity and purpose.

So, take the time to reflect on your experiences and identify what makes you truly happy and fulfilled. What moments have made you feel the most proud and satisfied? By answering these questions, you can uncover your personal values and create a solid foundation for your future. Remember, your values are a fundamental part of who you are and can guide you towards a life of purpose and fulfillment.

Other important aspects of aligning your purpose with your values is to establish a set of **standards** that you will always adhere to, no matter what. This means creating a personal code of conduct that will guide you in making decisions that align with your values and help you achieve your purpose.

For example, let's say you've identified your purpose as becoming a successful entrepreneur. One of your core values is honesty, and you believe that success should be earned through hard work and integrity, rather than deceit or unethical behavior. To align your purpose with this value, you may establish a standard that you will never engage in any form of theft, whether it be stealing from a competitor, cheating on your taxes, or even taking office supplies from your workplace.

Establishing these standards can help you stay on track and avoid temptation or situations that may compromise your values.

It gives you a clear set of guidelines to follow, and can also help you make decisions more easily. For example, if you're faced with a choice that may violate your code of conduct, you can quickly and confidently say "no" because it goes against your standards.

Having a set of standards can also help you build trust with others. When people know that you have a clear set of values and principles that you live by, they're more likely to trust you and do business with you. It can also help you build a positive reputation in your community, which can be invaluable when it comes to networking and building a successful career.

So, when it comes to aligning your purpose with your values, establishing standards is an essential step. By setting a clear code of conduct that aligns with your values and purpose, you can make decisions more easily, build trust with others, and create a roadmap for achieving your goals.

Now that you have reached the point of clarity with your self, purpose, values, and standards! It's time to take action and figure out what steps you need to take to achieve your purpose.

For instance, let's imagine your purpose is to climb a high mountain, like Mount Everest. The first step is to assess whether you have the necessary skills, education, or experience to tackle such a daunting task. If not, then what steps can you take to acquire the knowledge and training necessary for the climb?

Perhaps you need to research and learn about the different types of mountains, climbing techniques, and equipment necessary to succeed. Or maybe you need to talk to people who have already climbed such mountains to get their insights and advice.

It's also important to break down your ultimate goal into smaller, more manageable goals. For example, you may want to start by climbing smaller peaks to build up your skills and experience before attempting Mount Everest.

Furthermore, when setting goals, it's essential to align them with your values and standards. Ask yourself whether your goals are in accordance with your values and standards. If not, then it may not be the right goal for you to pursue.

By using the reverse engineering technique, you can create a career roadmap that aligns with your purpose, values, and standards. This technique involves breaking down your purpose into smaller, achievable goals, taking daily steps towards achieving them, and reflecting on your goals to make sure they align with your values and standards.

In summary, the reverse engineering technique involves identifying what you need to achieve your purpose, breaking it down into smaller goals, and taking daily steps towards achieving it. Reflecting on your goals and making sure they align with your values and standards is also crucial. With this approach, you can create a roadmap to achieve your ultimate career goals and fulfill your purpose.

Now It's time to find your true north. This term refers to the core values, passions, and strengths that align with your chosen career path, and it's the key to making fulfilling, meaningful, and purpose-driven career choices.

Many people focus on external factors, like salary or job security, when choosing a career path. While these are important, they can't substitute for the internal factors that drive your personal sense of fulfillment. By tapping into your true north, you'll discover what truly drives you and use it as a compass to guide your career choices.

Finding your true north isn't a one-time event, but an ongoing process of self-discovery and growth. Start by taking a deep dive into yourself and reflecting on what matters most to you. What are your personal values, strengths, and interests? Once you have a clear understanding of these, you can begin exploring career paths that align with them.

Keep in mind that your true north may evolve as you gain more experience and knowledge. So, stay open to new possibilities and be willing to adjust your career path as needed. By staying true to your inner compass, you'll find greater fulfillment and meaning in your career choices.

Your true North career options

Once not so long back, a family friend of mine was anxious about her daughter Moli, who had just completed her schooling and had no idea what she should do next. Moli was an average student who had completed her 12th with an average score. When her mother consulted me, I found out Moli had no particular interests, but she was a hard-working child with a definite personality and purpose. So, I advised Moli to enroll herself in any good university in any course for graduation. And asked her mother to invest in providing her tuitions that will help her prepare for CAT (Combined Aptitude test) to pursue an MBA from a reputed college. They followed my suggestion, and after her graduation, Moli cleared CAT with a fantastic result and now is part of a very prestigious college pursuing an MBA. The likes of Moli always make me remember the fact that not every child fits the same mold. In Moli's case, she walked on a narrow path that leads her to a brighter and wider opportunity. All the children out there are different with different interests and qualities, some with dreams and some who are yet to realize their identity, which why the formula to find their true potential also varies.

In Moli's case, she was not aware of her interests and inclinations, but with the right help and guidance, she found her identity. Are we just like Moli? Or do we have something we feel inclined towards? Below are given a few of the career options that are based on different fields of interest; these options consist of both conventional and unconventional ones. Shall we find out which career we relate to most?

16 Career Options for Mathematics Lovers

Most of us cringe at the thought of dealing with numbers. It's the time when turning blank or clueless. But there is a set of people whose life revolves around numbers, theorems, and calculations. While others may call them nerds, they delight in being better than the best. If mathematics is your true calling, you could try these career options.

1. **Mathematics Professor:** If you want to enjoy your love for math and remain in the academe, then you can choose to be a professor. You not only get to cultivate the seeds of the subjects in young minds but also carry on research and find new theories.
2. **Mathematician:** Mathematicians use advanced mathematical theories and principles to solve real-world problems. They work in a variety of industries, including engineering, finance, and technology.
3. **Actuary:** Actuaries use mathematical and statistical techniques to assess risk and determine the likelihood of events occurring. They work for insurance companies, consulting firms, and government agencies.
4. **Data analyst:** Data analysts collect, organize, and interpret large sets of data to identify patterns and trends. They work in a variety of industries, including finance, marketing, and healthcare.
5. **Statistician:** Statisticians use statistical methods to collect, analyze, and interpret data. They work in a variety of industries, including healthcare, government, and finance.

6. **Operations research analyst:** Operations research analysts use mathematical models to analyze complex problems and develop solutions. They work in a variety of industries, including healthcare, finance, and transportation.
7. **Cryptographer:** Cryptographers use mathematics and computer science to develop and analyze codes and ciphers. They work in a variety of industries, including government, military, and finance.
8. **Financial analyst:** Financial analysts use mathematical models and statistical analysis to evaluate financial data and make investment recommendations. They work for banks, investment firms, and corporations.
9. **Software developer:** Software developers use mathematical concepts and programming languages to design and develop computer software. They work in a variety of industries, including technology and finance.
10. **Research analyst:** Research analysts use mathematical models and statistical techniques to analyze data and identify trends. They work for research firms, government agencies, and corporations.
11. **Economist:** Economists use mathematical models to analyze data and develop economic policies. They work for government agencies, consulting firms, and research institutions.
12. **Computer scientist:** Computer scientists use mathematical principles to design and develop computer programs and software. They work in a variety of industries, including technology and finance.
13. **Engineer:** Engineers use mathematical principles to design, develop, and test products and systems. They work in a variety of industries, including aerospace, automotive, and electronics.
14. **Physicist:** Physicists use mathematical models to study the behavior of matter and energy. They work in a variety

of industries, including research institutions, government agencies, and universities.
15. **Biostatistician:** Biostatisticians use statistical methods to analyze data in the fields of medicine, public health, and biology. They work for hospitals, research institutions, and government agencies.
16. **Meteorologist:** Meteorologists use mathematical models and statistical techniques to forecast weather patterns. They work for government agencies, news organizations, and research institutions.

In summary, mathematics plays a vital role in a wide range of industries, and there are a variety of career paths available for those with a strong foundation in math.

10 Careers for people who wish to pursue Education

A career in education can be very fulfilling and rewarding, as it provides the opportunity to make a positive impact on the lives of others. There are many different paths you can take within the field of education, depending on your interests and skills. Here are some options:

1. **Teacher:** The most obvious career option in education is teaching. Teachers are responsible for imparting knowledge to students at various levels, ranging from elementary school to college. They create lesson plans, grade assignments, and manage classroom behavior.
2. **Curriculum Developer:** Curriculum developers design educational materials, including textbooks, lesson plans, and instructional software. They work with teachers and administrators to create materials that meet educational standards and promote learning.
3. **Educational Consultant:** Educational consultants provide advice and guidance to schools, districts, and other educational

organizations. They may help with curriculum development, teacher training, or school improvement efforts.
4. **Education Administrator:** Education administrators work in schools, colleges, and universities to oversee educational programs and manage staff. They may be responsible for budgeting, hiring, and curriculum development.
5. **School Counselor:** School counselors provide guidance and support to students, helping them to develop academic and personal skills. They may work with students one-on-one or in groups, and they may help with college applications, career planning, and other important life decisions.
6. **Educational Psychologist:** Educational psychologists study how people learn and develop, and they use this knowledge to create educational programs and materials. They may work in research or in schools, helping to identify and address learning challenges.
7. **Librarian:** Librarians help students and teachers find the resources they need to support their education. They manage collections of books and other materials, and they help users to navigate databases and other online resources.
8. **Special Education Teacher:** Special education teachers work with students who have a wide range of disabilities or learning challenges. They develop individualized education plans (IEPs) and provide specialized instruction and support.
9. **Online Instructor:** Online instructors teach classes over the internet, often to students who are located in different parts of the world. They may work for schools or universities, or they may teach courses independently.
10. **Adult Education Teacher:** Adult education teachers work with students who are over the age of 18 and are returning to school to complete their education or learn new skills. They may teach classes in basic literacy, English as a second language, or vocational training.

11. **Educational Technology Specialist:** Educational technology specialists work to integrate technology into the classroom, helping teachers use tools like interactive whiteboards, tablets, and online learning platforms to enhance student learning.

7 Careers in psychology and Maths

A career in psychology and maths can offer a wide range of opportunities. Here are some career options in both fields:

1. **Psychometrician:** Psychometricians use statistical methods to develop and analyze psychological tests and assessments. They may work in academic research, government agencies, or private companies.
2. **Research Psychologist:** Research psychologists conduct studies and experiments to investigate human behavior and mental processes. They may work in academic research, government agencies, or private companies.
3. **Neuropsychologist:** Neuropsychologists study how the brain affects behavior and mental processes. They may work in hospitals, rehabilitation centers, or private practice.
4. **Data Analyst:** Data analysts use statistical methods to analyze data, including psychological research data. They may work in a variety of industries, including healthcare, finance, and marketing.
5. **Actuary:** Actuaries use mathematical models to assess risk and develop strategies to manage it. They may work in insurance companies, government agencies, or consulting firms.
6. **Financial Analyst:** Financial analysts use mathematical models to analyze financial data and make investment recommendations. They may work in finance, banking, or consulting.

7. **Operations Research Analyst:** Operations research analysts use mathematical models to optimize business processes and solve complex problems. They may work in a variety of industries, including healthcare, transportation, and logistics.
8. **Statistician:** Statisticians use statistical methods to collect, analyze, and interpret data. They may work in a variety of industries, including healthcare, government, and research.

There are many other career paths in psychology and math, but these are some of the most common. Whether you choose to pursue a career in psychology or math, or a combination of both, there are many opportunities to make a meaningful impact in your field.

5 Career for those who love Home Science

Home Science is a diverse academic discipline that extends beyond cooking and tailoring, encompassing the study of various aspects of homes and families to enhance the satisfaction of every family member through the effective utilization of resources. Despite the existence of several misconceptions, it is crucial to promote Home Science as a professional course that offers students numerous opportunities to build a successful career.

Upon choosing Home Science as a subject after 12th, students can pursue various career paths, some of which are as follows:

1. **Nutrition Expert:** If you have a passion for nutrition, then Home Science is an excellent subject choice for you. Pursuing a B.Sc and M.Sc degree in Home Science/Food and Nutrition/Clinical Nutrition and Dietetics/Applied Nutrition can help you become a dietitian. You can also take the RD (Registered Dietitian) exam to become a certified professional dietitian.

2. **Child Caregiver:** A career in Child Care is ideal for those who enjoy working with children and are interested in their overall development. You can explore education in this field, such as a diploma or masters in early childhood care and education, to become a child caregiver.
3. **Food Scientist:** If you are interested in the science behind food, then a career as a food scientist is a great option for you. After completing your BA Home Science, pursuing a Masters's degree in Food Science and Technology can help you become a food scientist. You can secure jobs in various government laboratories, authorities like BIS and FSSAI, or university research posts like CFTRI, ICAR, DFRL, etc.
4. **Chef/Cook:** A degree in Hotel Management culinary specialization or a certificate course in food production is the way to go if you love cooking and want to pursue a career in culinary arts. You can also sit for hospitality entrance exams like the National Council of Hotel Management JEE to become a professional chef, which has a broad scope worldwide.
5. **Teacher:** With a Bachelor's in Home Science, doing a B.Ed. will be helpful in becoming a teacher with a broad scope. After completing your masters, you can even become a professor.

The scope after BA Home Science is continuously rising, with opportunities available in areas such as Fashion Journalism, Commercial Restaurants, Food Industry, Specialized Cooking, Hospitals, Food Preservation, Hotels, Manufacturing Industries, Sales Promotion of Food Items, Textile Businesses, and Tourist Resorts. Thus, it is essential to dispel the stereotypes and seize the numerous opportunities available in Home Science to build a successful career.

5 Career Options for Hindi Lovers

Many of us ignore Hindi calling it the language of the poor or uneducated, completely ignoring the fact that it's the mode that first strikes us when we want to convey our thoughts and ideas. There's a fluency attached to it. If the language interests you and you wish to pursue a career after graduating in the subject, here are five career options for you that pay well.

1. **Teaching:** Like any other subject, Hindi teachers are paid well not only within the national boundaries but also at the global level. CBSE syllabus based schools make it a point to have Hindi as a compulsory subject at the primary level.
2. **Mass Communication:** With the broad reach of media and FM, there are massive opportunities for Hindi lovers. Be it print media or digital media, Hindi Graduates are in demand because they gain the advantage of speaking the language of the masses.
3. **Parliamentary Jobs:** Hindi graduates are also hired for the post of Hindi assistants and parliamentary reporters. And being a government job, it pays you well.
4. **Translator:** Hindi graduates also find ample opportunities as translators or interpreters and proofreaders. With a good command of the language, you could also find a lucrative offer in this field.
5. **Bank Jobs:** Securing a post in banks is not that easy, and Hindi can never be an obstacle in your path if you want to pick a bank job. Many banks like the Institute of Banking Personnel Selection require Hindi language officers.

7 Career Options for Literature/ linguistics Lovers

People believe that literature students get away with reading novels – a pastime turned into full-time work. But it's not that easy a task. Right from reading between the lines, understanding the period in which it was written (all the factors like social, political, economic) to dis/agreeing with the critics, they do it all. And it is not a bed of roses. But the hard work pays off. So, if you are a literature lover, you could define your path.

1. **Teacher:** The best way to use your knowledge is to share it with young minds. As a teacher, you can make a tremendous change in the way the students think.
2. **Journalism:** Journalism allows the students to explore the real world. From writing, researching, and reporting, you get to do all exciting stuff.
3. **Publishing:** Entering into publishing is like a dream come true for literature students because this is the home to some of the exciting novels that reach our hands.
4. **Public Relations:** As a PR, your work is to maintain a favorable public image of firm/ firms. This allows you to carry out research work, write and publicize their work, and maintain a harmonious relationship with their clients.
5. **Authors:** Having lived in different centuries, understood various genres, and walked with numerous authors, you can step into their shoes and tell your tale to the world.
6. **Bloggers:** With the far reach of technology and its benefits, many firms hire bloggers to market their services and products. Your work as a blogger would require you to plan content schedules, come up with new ideas for the blogs, monitor traffic, and analyze feedback.
7. **Government Jobs:** There's a vast ocean of opportunities here. From being an editor, communication officer to handling NGOs, you can carve your path.

5 Career Options for History Lovers

History buffs often immerse themselves in the magnificence of the past world, secrets of the dead, and other mysteries. If watching O'Connell and family fight the mummies made your eyes pop out, then you could also try out these fantastic career options specially made for history lovers.

1. **Genealogist:** If the past world makes you nostalgic and you are amazed by their style of living, you could give this choice a shot. Your work would involve studying how people in different eras lived and how it has impacted our present-day lifestyle. Genealogists work with individuals or families to trace their backgrounds and research their ancestors, using documents like birth and marriage certificates, court records, obituaries, and more.
2. **Museum Technician:** If studying fossils has interested you, then you could try being a museum technician. They work with fossils and skeletons, art, books, and other artifacts, and prepare them for research and exhibits. And there is never a dull moment in their lives.
3. **Underwater Archaeologist:** Underwater archaeologists study and examine shipwrecks, sunken aircraft, historical remains, and artifacts found in marine and once-inhabited areas that have since become submerged due to natural disasters. And if luck favors you, you might even strike gold in treasure hunts.
4. **Museum Curators:** Museum requires people with a historical background to fit into various roles like archivists, curators, and tour guides to maintain ancient artifacts. Museum curators get to live at their favorite place and interact with like-minded people and infect them with their love for history and other objects from the past world. Plus, you get to earn well too.
5. **Teaching:** History buff can always work as educationists and impart knowledge to the young students to create an impact on their minds about the glories of the lost world. This profession allows you to be in direct contact with the present and teach about the past.

5 Career Options for Those Who Love Political Science

A common stereotype concerning political science majors is that they either become politicians or teachers. However, this myth needs to be busted. Take a look at the possible career options for people who would like to go for political science honors.

1. **Lawyer:** One of the most common lines for a graduate in political science is to pursue a degree in law. Political science knowledge gives lawyers the required edge over others.
2. **Print/Television Journalism:** Knowledge of politics is always beneficial if you are thinking of going into journalism. But you also need to be expressive and convincing.
3. **Public Policy Analyst:** Since every year, some new policies are launched by the government, policy analysts try to analyze and review these policies and their implementation. They then determine the loopholes in the policies and give the possible corrective measures.
4. **Bureaucrats:** The main job of the bureaucrat is to manage government policies, law, and order. So a degree in political science provides an understanding of the functioning of the government machinery.
5. **Diplomat:** A diplomat has to negotiate deals, treaties, and act as an intermediary between two or more states or organizations. They are representative of their country or organization and have to discuss the political, legal, economic, and cultural dimensions of a treaty. Therefore, political science only adds to their theoretical knowledge. However, as a diplomat, one also needs to have strong negotiating and persuasive skills.

12 Career Options for People Who Love Geography

Someone who loves geography will always enjoy studying and exploring places and their topography. They will try to understand why a particular area has a different weather pattern and also specific typical characteristics that are associated with that place. They will try to establish a relationship between the environment and human beings. So if you are one of the few people who love geography and are willing to pursue a career in this field, then read further.

1. **Geoscientist:** The study of the earth's structure and its composition is called geosciences. A geoscientist has to study the universe and its processes to find the functioning of the earth's system and its effects on life forms. The methods by which natural resources develop, soil and fertility variation, the various sources of energy, varying weather conditions across regions, and how climate change affects human beings, oceans, and their protection, are only a few of the areas that a geoscientist explores.
2. **Hydrologist:** Water is found in three different forms on earth—liquid, ice, and steam. A hydrologist has to study the processes through which water transforms into its different states and also the various water resources found on earth, which can serve social purposes.
3. **Meteorologist:** A meteorologist studies the climate and atmosphere and the changes it undergoes from time to time. They also explore how climate change will affect living beings in the future and suggest ways to mitigate climate-related disasters. There is a vast scope in this area, as both government and private agencies employ meteorologists.
4. **Cartographer:** The word 'cartography' literally means writing maps. So the job of the cartographer is to study and make maps. This job requires high creativity and scientific skills. A cartographer can work for a government or private publisher/agency which produces atlases or require plans.
5. **Urban/City Planners:** Due to the process of rapid urbanization, the need for urban planners is growing. An urban planner has to analyze landscapes and develop plans

for how and where development programs ought and could be implemented. They have to examine not only the geographical aspects of an area but also the cultural and historical elements so that development is practical, sustainable, and environment friendly.

6. **Geographer:** A geographer studies the physical and cultural features of the earth's surface, such as landforms, climates, populations, and economic activities.
7. **Environmental Consultant:** An environmental consultant provides advice on environmental issues to companies, organizations, and governments to help minimize the impact of human activities on natural resources and ecosystems
8. **Geographic Information Systems (GIS) Specialist:** A GIS specialist uses computer software to analyze, store, and manipulate geographic data to help solve problems related to environmental management, urban planning, and public health.
9. **Landscape Architect:** A landscape architect designs and plans outdoor spaces, such as parks, gardens, and campuses, to create functional and aesthetically pleasing environments.
10. **Climatologist:** A climatologist studies patterns and changes in the earth's climate, including weather patterns, atmospheric conditions, and the impact of climate change on ecosystems.
11. **Geospatial Analyst:** A geospatial analyst uses geographic data to analyze and interpret spatial patterns, relationships, and trends, often for government agencies or private companies.
12. **International Development Specialist:** An international development specialist works on projects related to economic and social development in other countries, often for government agencies or non-profit organizations, with a focus on issues such as poverty, sustainability, and human rights.

5 Career Options for Those Who Love Economics

If you thought that economics was the most boring subject, then think again because economics is a science that helps us comprehend society.

People who love economics realize that to understand the culture means to unravel its underlying economics. A major in economics gives one a whole lot of options in this field.

1. **Financial Risk Analyst:** In a business, the job of a financial risk analyst is crucial as he is the one who analyses the potential financial risks that are posed to the company and its assets. They have to monitor market behavior, government policies, and customer behavior to analyze the risks involved. There are many areas of specialization in this field, like credit risk specialists, market risk specialists, operational risk specialists, and regulatory risk analysts.
2. **Economist:** An economist is an expert on economic theories and also real economic issues like markets, demand, and supply, deficits, budgets, risks, savings, debts, inflation, policies, etc. They also recommend what would be the best course of action in a situation. As an economist, one can be employed in academia, in financial institutions, or in the government sector.
3. **Insurance Agent:** An insurance agent has to engage with people and sell different types of insurances that can range from health, life to property. As an insurance agent, one can work independently or work for a company for compensation.
4. **Business Journalist:** If you have a degree in economics and also have relatively excellent writing skills, then becoming a business journalist will be quite lucrative. The feat to express economic terms to the public is a rare quality, and business journalism requires such people.

5. **Chartered Accountant:** A chartered accountant works for companies or the government sector and helps them in managing the financial and business economy. However, to become a chartered accountant, one has to get a professional degree in Chartered Accountancy.

8 Career options for those who like Accounts and Business

For anyone who thinks Accounts and Business Studies was only for nerds or are not fun, you should think again. Both of these fields are interrelated and require a vast amount of understanding and presence of mind. Accounts for some is like jigsaw puzzles that they have to add up and solve to find out a bigger picture. And the 'fear of risk' involved in business for some becomes a thrill factor along with the power and authority it brings.

1. **Chartered Accountant** – CA is one of the most respected and challenging career options, especially for commerce students. However, humanities and science students can also opt for it by clearing the set of exams conducted by the Indian Chartered Accountants Institute (ICAI). The work involves either working in the accounts department or acting as a private advisor in any organization. A Chartered Accountant is also allowed to open his own CA Firm. Significant fields of work of a CA includes auditing, taxation, transfer pricing, assurance services, investment banking,
2. **Chartered Financial Analyst-** provides students and professionals with a strong foundation for careers in Investment Banking, Equity Research, Capital Market, Portfolio Management, Corporate Finance, etc.
3. **Cost Management Accounting** – the work of CMA is to improve and maximize a company's profitability by managing expenses and revenues. It helps in determining the cost

involved in the business, identifying the places of profit and loss, and is also an essential part of budget planning.
4. **Financial Manager-** responsible for the financial health of an organization, Financial Manager produce direct investment activities, financial reports, and also develop plans and strategies for the long-term financial goals. They work to deal with business advisors and top executives, helping them in making significant decisions.
5. **Financial Advisor-** the work of a Financial Advisor, includes providing financial advice and guidance to the customer for compensation, investment management, tax planning, and estate planning. Their range of services comprises from portfolio management to insurance products as they act as a one-stop-shop.
6. **Entrepreneur-** a popular career option amongst anyone who loves taking risks and is interested in business. Entrepreneurship is often considered a road less traveled because of the risk factors that are ever so present. The person who can envision the excitement in fear of failure can opt for entrepreneurship in any field.
7. **Company Secretary-** the role of the company secretary, involves providing support to the board of directors, managing administrative affairs, take care of corporate governance and even legal matters of the company. CS not only is a high position but also gives innumerable challenging situations.
8. **Business Reporter-** work involves analyzing companies and industries and create content based on their research but just like reporters. They have fantastic communication skills and explicit knowledge of everything going on in the business world.

5 Career Choices for Those Who Love Chemistry

Chemistry is not just about mixing compounds but also identifying the underlying structure of things. Everything around us, whether it's the food we eat or the things we use in everyday life, have a particular composition and properties they exhibit. If you like studying these structures and composition, then the following career options will be open to you.

1. **Chemical Engineering:** A chemical engineer has to analyze chemical compounds and their structures and develop materials that are safe and can be used in various fields like food, agriculture, medicine, textiles, manufacturing, etc.
2. **Cheminformatics:** It is the combination of the two fields- chemistry and computer science. Cheminformatics uses computer programs to solve chemical problems and use databases to evolve and use complex chemical structures in the most effective way, which can then be used in various fields.
3. **Biochemistry:** An amalgamation of biology and chemistry, biochemists have to study chemical processes that take place in a living organism.
4. **Toxicology:** A field that studies the adverse effects that a chemical compound or substance has on organisms and how the body reacts to the material at an appropriate dose. When a new compound is developed, it is often tested for its safety standards and the effects it has on the environment, and this is where the work of the toxicologist comes in.
5. **Forensic Chemistry:** This is a combination of chemistry and criminal investigation. A forensic chemist has to analyze certain pieces of evidence like blood samples, clothes, etc., found at a crime scene and give possible explanations that may assist the case.

5 Career Options for Those Who Love Biology

If you thought that opting for biology as a subject in high school meant treading the path to being a doctor, then you might think again. Careers in biology are vast in scope, and there are various choices in medical sciences and in biology itself that might seem attractive to students of biology.

1. **Microbiologist:** To study microscopic forms of life like fungi, bacteria, viruses, and protozoa is called microbiology. The job of the microbiologist is to study the growth of these organisms in a particular environment. A microbiologist might be employed in one of the following sectors- medicine, environment, food, agriculture, etc. In the medical industry, a microbiologist may be involved in studying diseases and their causes. In the agricultural sector, the microbiologist explores plant microbes and the causes of plant diseases.
2. **Biotechnology:** This field involves not only biology but also a certain amount of engineering. When technology is developed through the study of the biological processes of organisms, it ultimately helps in making our lives better. For example, useful bacteria are used to create food products that are good for health. Biotechnologists also come up with vaccines and develop technologies that will help reduce environmental damages.
3. **Genetics:** If you have considerable interest in studying how organisms evolved, then this option is perfect for you. As a geneticist, one has to study how hereditary and evolution works and how biological information is passed through the DNA.
4. **Environmental Biologist:** This field is vast and encompasses various areas like chemistry, biology, ecology, etc. An ecological biologist has to study the ecosystem and the biological processes of a particular area. After which they come up with solutions for environmental damages and sustainable development.

5. **Animal Behavior:** Animal behavior and its causes, animal psychology, and the evolution of physical, biological instincts are some of the concerns of an animal behavior biologist. They also study the evolution of these instincts and how they might have transformed over generations. Many specialists in this area go for research on animal behavior conducted by various organizations and institutes.

6 Career Options If You Love Physics

The way we understand the world and its workings today has primarily been the contribution made by physics. Whether it's explaining the laws underlying the structures of matter, how energy is transferred and transformed, to how we can use physics for communications and for making everyday life better with gadgets, physics encompasses all. For people who love physics and are willing to go one step further, the following career options might seem suitable.

1. **Astrophysicist-** being an astrophysicist means that one tries to find answers to some of the most sought after questions in human history, relating to the birth and origin of the universe including stars, galaxies, and other objects like asteroids, black holes, quasars, dark matter, dark energy, cosmic rays, etc. using theoretical and applied physics.
2. **Astronaut-** an astronaut is a trained person who has to become a crew member of a spacecraft and often man it once it has been launched.
3. **Satellite Engineer-** Artificial satellites have become the most critical part of human civilization because they not only help monitor the earth from space by studying the weather conditions and alerting us about possible threats but are crucial in communications and navigations. A satellite engineer has to design programs that control an orbiting satellite.

4. **Robotics Engineering-** A branch of mechanical, electrical, and computer engineering, robotics deals with constructing robots that will follow specific commands to complete a given task. This field requires a lot of original thinking and creativity because this field is becoming extremely competitive.
5. **Architect-** If building structures is your forte then physics will be one of the areas of your interest. Without physics, the existence of structures like the Stonehenge (United kingdom), the pyramids of Giza(Egypt), or the BurjKhalifa(UAE), the tallest building in the world, would not have been possible because physics lies at the base of any structural design.
6. **Artificial Intelligence-** this is an emerging field and deals with making machines or software that can think and make judgments that ensure maximum success, by predicting the environment and behavior and without any human guidance.

30 Career Specializations in Psychology

Solving the mystery around human beings and their evolution depends on unraveling what constitutes the human brain and its functioning. Psychology is the science of studying what defines human emotions and thinking. With a major in psychology, you can later specialize in the many areas that are available in this field.

1. **Clinical Psychologist:** Certain mental and behavioral disorders need medical attention. The task of a clinical psychologist is to assess and analyze and treat a person who suffers from these disorders, which often hampers learning, relationships, and leads to depression.
2. **Child Psychologist:** Children and adolescents have diverse needs and require a different kind of care because their thinking processes differ from those of adults. Child psychologists study child behavior, development, and

growth. They also identify children with special needs or those who require specific attention.
3. **Rehabilitation Psychologist:** Rehabilitation is a therapy that aims to restore a person to their normal emotional state and thinking capabilities. When people suffer from trauma, loss, illness, disabilities, or addictions (drugs, alcohol), then the role of rehabilitation comes up because these experiences make people susceptible to depression and other mental disorders.
4. **Counselor:** A counselor hears the problems of clients and offers them solutions. They have excellent listening skills and a problem-solving attitude. There are many types of counselors, like career counselors, marriage counselors, etc.
5. **Criminal Psychology:** Criminals are also human beings, and understanding why and how people are driven to commit crimes is the main aim of this specialization. The intentions, the reactions of criminal after the crime is also a part of the study in this specialization. As a criminal psychologist, one is often required to cooperate with the police and court.
6. **Consumer Psychologist:** Living in a society that is driven by consumerism, the importance of understanding what drives people to buy, and follow a particular fashion, and make choices are important to businesses across the world. The main aim of the consumer psychologist is to analyze and predict consumer behavior.
7. **Forensic Psychologist:** Forensic psychologists apply psychological principles to legal issues and may work in law enforcement, corrections, or the courts. They may also conduct evaluations of individuals involved in legal cases, such as criminal defendants or witnesses.
8. **School Psychologist:** School psychologists work in educational settings and focus on helping students with academic and behavioral issues. They may assess students

for learning disabilities, provide counseling and therapy, and consult with teachers and parents.
9. **Industrial-Organizational Psychologist:** Industrial-organizational psychologists apply psychological principles to the workplace, focusing on issues such as employee selection, training, and development, as well as organizational development and change management.
10. **Neuropsychologist:** Neuropsychologists study the relationship between the brain and behavior, using advanced technology to assess and diagnose individuals with neurological disorders, such as traumatic brain injury, Alzheimer's disease, and stroke.
11. **Social Psychologist:** Social psychologists study how people interact with one another and how social factors influence behavior, attitudes, and beliefs. They may work in academia, government, or the private sector.
12. **Developmental Psychologist:** Developmental psychologists study the changes that occur across the lifespan, from infancy to old age, and may focus on areas such as cognitive, social, and emotional development.
13. **Sports Psychologist:** Sports psychologists work with athletes, coaches, and teams to help them improve performance, manage stress, and cope with the mental and emotional demands of competition.
14. **Health Psychologist:** Health psychologists focus on the intersection of psychological and physical health, studying factors such as lifestyle, behavior change, and the impact of stress on health outcomes. They may work in clinical or research settings.
15. **Environmental Psychologist:** An environmental psychologist studies the interaction between individuals and their physical and social environment. They may apply their knowledge to improve urban planning, transportation design, and sustainable development.

16. **Military Psychologist:** A military psychologist provides mental health services to members of the military and their families. They may also work with veterans to help them adjust to civilian life after their service.
17. **Research Psychologist:** A research psychologist conducts scientific research to understand human behavior and mental processes. They use various research methods to study behavior, cognition, emotions, and attitudes, and may work in academic, government, or private research institutions.
18. **Educational Psychologist:** An educational psychologist applies psychological principles and theories to improve learning outcomes and educational practices. They work with teachers, students, and educational institutions to identify and address learning and behavioral difficulties, develop effective teaching strategies, and design educational programs.
19. **Community Psychologist:** A community psychologist works with individuals and groups in community settings to promote social justice, prevent social problems, and improve community well-being. They use a range of strategies, such as community organizing, program development, and advocacy, to address issues such as poverty, violence, and discrimination.
20. **Media Psychologist:** A media psychologist studies the effects of media on human behavior, attitudes, and emotions. They examine how media influences individuals and society, and may work in fields such as advertising, journalism, and entertainment to develop media content that is responsible and effective.
21. **Geropsychologist:** A geropsychologist specializes in the mental health needs of older adults. They may work in nursing homes, hospitals, or community centers, providing assessment, treatment, and support to older adults with cognitive or emotional challenges.

22. **Positive Psychologist:** A positive psychologist focuses on the study of positive emotions, traits, and behaviors, with the goal of promoting well-being and human flourishing. They may work in academic or private settings, developing interventions and programs to help individuals and communities to build resilience, optimism, and happiness.
23. **Behavioral Psychologist:** A behavioral psychologist studies the relationship between behavior and the environment. They focus on observable behavior and use techniques such as reinforcement, punishment, and conditioning to modify behavior and promote positive outcomes.
24. **Political Psychologist:** A political psychologist studies the psychological factors that influence political attitudes and behavior. They examine the role of personality, emotion, cognition, and social influence in political decision-making, and may work in fields such as public opinion research, political campaigns, or government policy.
25. **Quantitative Psychologist:** A quantitative psychologist uses statistical and mathematical methods to analyze data and solve problems in psychology. They may work in academic or research settings, developing and applying new statistical models and methods to address research questions.
26. **Family Therapist:** A family therapist helps families and couples to improve their relationships and resolve conflicts. They provide counseling, support, and education to help families develop effective communication, problem-solving, and coping skills.
27. **Marriage and Couples Therapist:** A marriage and couples therapist specializes in helping couples to strengthen their relationships and overcome challenges. They provide counseling, therapy, and support to help couples improve communication, intimacy, and trust.
28. **Addiction Counselor:** An addiction counselor helps individuals and families to overcome substance abuse and

addiction. They provide counseling, therapy, and support to help clients recover from addiction, develop coping skills, and prevent relapse.
29. **Art Therapist:** An art therapist uses art and creative expression to promote emotional, cognitive, and social growth. They work with individuals and groups to help them explore and express their feelings, thoughts, and experiences through various art forms.
30. **Music Therapist:** A music therapist uses music to promote physical, emotional, and cognitive well-being. They work with individuals and groups to help them achieve therapeutic goals, such as reducing

14 Careers for working for cause of Non communicable disease

If a person is keen on working in noncommunicable diseases, they may opt for the following careers:

1. **Epidemiologist:** An epidemiologist studies patterns and causes of diseases in a population. They may focus on noncommunicable diseases and work to understand their prevalence and risk factors.
2. **Health Educator:** A health educator develops and implements programs to educate individuals and communities about noncommunicable diseases, their prevention, and treatment.
3. **Public Health Policy Analyst:** A public health policy analyst analyzes and develops policies related to noncommunicable diseases. They work to ensure that policies are evidence-based and effective in preventing and treating these diseases.
4. **Medical Researcher:** Medical researchers conduct studies to understand the causes, prevention, and treatment of noncommunicable diseases. They may work in a laboratory or a clinical setting.

5. **Clinical Trials Manager:** A clinical trials manager oversees clinical trials of new treatments for noncommunicable diseases. They ensure that the trials are conducted ethically and effectively.
6. **Health Data Analyst:** A health data analyst collects, analyzes, and interprets data related to noncommunicable diseases. They may work for government agencies, research organizations, or healthcare providers.
7. **Healthcare Administrator:** A healthcare administrator manages healthcare facilities, programs, and services. They may work to improve access to care for individuals with noncommunicable diseases and ensure that resources are used effectively.
8. **Nutritionist/Dietitian:** A professional who advises people on how to eat healthily and manage their diet in order to prevent non-communicable diseases.
9. **Occupational Therapist:** A healthcare professional who helps people to recover or develop the skills necessary to lead independent and fulfilling lives, particularly after an injury or illness.
10. **Physical Therapist:** A healthcare professional who helps people to recover from injury or illness by using exercise and other techniques to improve physical strength and mobility.
11. **Public Health Advocate:** A person who works to raise awareness of non-communicable diseases and promote policies that encourage healthy lifestyles and prevent the spread of these diseases.
12. **Social Worker:** A professional who provides support to individuals and families who are dealing with a range of social, emotional, or economic problems that can contribute to non-communicable diseases.
13. **Sports Medicine Physician:** A healthcare professional who specializes in the diagnosis, treatment, and prevention of injuries and illnesses related to sports and physical activity.

14. **Wellness Coach:** A professional who works with individuals to help them achieve their goals for health and well-being, including weight loss, stress reduction, and disease prevention.

19 Careers for creative people

Hey there, creative minds! Have you ever felt out of place in academic settings and unsure of what career paths to take? Well, fear not because there are plenty of exciting career options for you to explore! Whether you're a celebrity or a struggler, there is something for everyone. Let's dive into a few careers that cater to your creative nature:

1. Are you a tech-savvy, creative thinker? A **mobile designer** might be the perfect job for you! As a mobile designer, you'll be responsible for creating user-friendly interfaces for mobile devices. You'll need to understand how customers use technology and come up with innovative ideas to make their experience seamless and intuitive.
2. If you have a passion for software and enjoy problem-solving, then **software engineering** might be the career for you. As a software engineer, you'll work with a team of programmers to develop and maintain high-quality software products. You'll be responsible for designing, testing, and creating products that meet the needs of clients or employers.
3. The face of a business is its brand. A **brand manager** is responsible for ensuring that a company's brand accurately reflects its values, voice, and products to consumers. They develop marketing strategies based on research and testing to align with the company's goals, and work with creative teams to execute these campaigns across various mediums.
4. As a **business development manager**, you'll be responsible for identifying growth opportunities and developing

marketing and sales strategies to help your company succeed. You'll work with clients and partners to create new business relationships, and oversee all aspects of the sales process to ensure successful outcomes.

5. Have you ever received an email from a brand that made you want to buy their product? An **email marketing specialist** is the creative mind behind those effective campaigns. They use their skills to create compelling email campaigns that engage and convert recipients into customers.

6. **Product designers** are responsible for creating innovative and practical products that meet the needs of consumers. They work with engineers, marketers, and executives to develop new products and improve existing ones. Think of the iPhone - product designers help create new models with features that consumers will love.

7. **SEO specialists** focus on improving website rankings on search engines like Google and Bing. They use their creative skills to create unique and engaging content that stands out from competitors. As an SEO specialist, you'll be responsible for researching popular keywords and developing content that reflects that research.

8. If you have a passion for animation or illustration, then becoming an **animator or illustrator** might be the perfect career for you. These creative professionals bring stories to life through visual mediums such as movies, music videos, and advertisements. Whether you choose to specialize in hand-drawing, 3D design, or CGI, there's a world of possibilities for you in this exciting field.

9. Are you a visionary who loves to come up with new and innovative ideas? Then being a **creative director** might just be the perfect career for you! You will be responsible for developing and implementing the creative vision for a company or project while overseeing other creatives such as

graphic designers, photographers, fashion designers, interior designers, and writers.

10. Do you have a passion for using visual elements to communicate ideas? As a **graphic designer**, you'll get to use your creative skills to create designs for various media platforms using typography, images, colors, shapes, and other design techniques.
11. If you have a knack for creating and maintaining the look, feel, and functionality of websites, then being a **web developer** might be for you! You'll get to use your programming skills to write code that tells the website how it should look and function.
12. Do you have a way with words and love to persuade people? A **copywrite**r is responsible for writing persuasive and compelling text for advertisements, brochures, website content, and more.
13. A **marketing director** plans and develops strategies for the promotion of products and services offered by their company. As a creative, you'll have an eye for detail and storytelling that can help you create campaigns that appeal to specific audiences.
14. Do you have a strong understanding of what your customers and shareholders want or need? A **digital marketing manager** creates and develops strategies for the promotion of products and services offered by their company on online channels such as Facebook, Twitter, Google AdWords, and more.
15. As a **UX designer**, you'll design user interfaces for software programs such as mobile apps and websites so that they're easy to navigate on any device. You'll have a strong understanding of how people interact with digital products to create an efficient and user-friendly interface.
16. A **UX researcher** investigates the experiences that people have with products and services offered by their company.

They are data-driven workers who should have a strong understanding of how people interact with technology.
17. If you have a knack for creating sound and video projects for television, film, or web-based media, then being a **video producer** might be perfect for you! You'll be responsible for overseeing everything from pre-production planning through post-production editing on any given project.
18. As a **social media specialist**, you'll manage the day-to-day aspects of a company's presence on platforms like Facebook, Twitter, and more. You'll be responsible for creating content that engages customers while also driving traffic back to your website, brand, or store location.
19. As a **technical writer**, you'll create manuals and other written materials that explain how products work. You must have a deep understanding of the product to explain it clearly and concisely.

Careers for student pursuing economics with Humanities

As an educator, I always encourage my students to think carefully about their career paths and make informed decisions. Recently, one of my students was considering taking economics with maths in the humanities stream, and it got me thinking - what difference does this combination really make?

As the American ambassador once said, John Kenneth rightly said, "Economics is extremely useful as a form of employment for economists." But what does that mean for my student and others like him? Well, I did some research and here's what I found:

From a job perspective, the employment rates in economics are predicted to grow by a whopping 78% from 2023-2031. That's right, you read that correctly - 78%! Currently, there are over 10,000 job openings in this field, which is a testament to its growing demand.

The employment rate under economics in the year 2021 stands at 16,900, whereas by 2031, the predicted stats stand at 17,800, which is a good and fast-paced transition. According to the stats, 95.6% of people with a degree in economics are employed and earning good numbers.

But what are the top careers in economics, you ask? Well, there are many! Here are just a few examples:

1. **Actuarial Analyst** - These professionals use statistical models to analyze the financial impact of risk and uncertainty, typically for insurance companies.
2. **Economist** - These individuals research and analyze economic issues, often to make predictions about future economic trends.
3. **External/internal Auditor** - Auditors ensure the accuracy and integrity of financial statements and compliance with relevant regulations.
4. **Data Analyst** - These professionals analyze and interpret large sets of data to identify trends and make recommendations for action.
5. **Risk Manager** - These individuals identify and assess potential risks to a company and develop strategies to mitigate them.
6. **Statistician** - Statisticians design and conduct experiments or surveys, analyze data, and interpret results.
7. **Investment Analyst** - These professionals research and evaluate investment opportunities, often for investment banks or asset management firms.
8. **Stockbroker** - Stockbrokers buy and sell securities on behalf of clients, often providing investment advice as well.

And that's not all! With a degree in economics, you could also pursue careers in the management sector, academics, government sector, administration, banking, or the public sector. The opportunities are truly endless.

So, for any student considering a career in economics, my advice would be to go for it! With the predicted growth in employment rates and numerous career opportunities, it's a field that's definitely worth considering. Who knows? You could be the next top economist or investment analyst!

11 Careers in Commerce without Maths

If you're looking for a career in the world of commerce but are not inclined towards mathematics, worry not! There are plenty of exciting and challenging career paths available to you. Here are a few options to consider:

1. Firstly, there's the role of a **Business Development Manager**. These professionals work to expand a company's customer base, partnerships, and overall revenue. They focus on building relationships and identifying opportunities for growth and expansion.
2. Another option is that of a **Marketing Manager**. These professionals develop and execute marketing strategies to promote a company's products or services. They conduct market research, develop advertising campaigns, and manage the marketing budget.
3. If you're interested in people management, then the role of a **Human Resources Manager** could be an excellent fit. In this position, you'd oversee the recruitment, training, and development of a company's employees. You'd also manage employee benefits, compensation, and ensure compliance with labor laws.
4. **Sales Managers** are responsible for overseeing a company's sales team and achieving sales targets and revenue goals. They develop sales strategies, identify new business opportunities, and manage customer relationships.

5. **Public Relations Managers** work to maintain a company's reputation and communicate with the public, media, and other stakeholders. They develop public relations strategies, manage media relations, and coordinate events and other public-facing activities.
6. **Financial Advisors** work with individuals and businesses to create financial plans, manage investments, and provide guidance on financial decisions. They focus on helping clients achieve their financial goals and plan for the future.
7. **Operations Managers** oversee a company's day-to-day operations and work to improve efficiency, productivity, and profitability. They develop and implement operational strategies, manage resources, and monitor performance metrics.
8. **Customer Service Managers** ensure customer satisfaction and loyalty by overseeing a company's customer service team. They develop customer service strategies, train and manage customer service representatives, and manage customer complaints and inquiries.
9. **Supply Chain Managers** oversee the production and distribution of a company's products or services. They manage logistics, procurement, inventory, and supplier relationships to optimize the supply chain for maximum efficiency and profitability.
10. And if you're interested in the rapidly-growing world of e-commerce, you might consider the role of an **E-commerce Manager**. These professionals oversee a company's online sales and digital presence, develop and execute e-commerce strategies, manage online marketing and advertising campaigns, and optimize the user experience for online customers.
11. The role of a **Company Secretary (CS)** is an excellent career option for those who are interested in corporate governance and have a strong legal and regulatory understanding. A CS

is a senior-level executive who acts as a legal advisor and is responsible for ensuring that a company complies with all legal and regulatory requirements. To become a Company Secretary, one must have a degree in commerce, law, or business administration, followed by a CS course. The CS course is conducted by the Institute of Company Secretaries of India (ICSI), and consists of three levels of examinations. A CS can work in a variety of organizations, including public companies, private companies, government organizations, and non-profit organizations. The demand for CS professionals is on the rise, and the salary package for a CS can be quite attractive.

12. A career as a **Certified Management Accountant (CMA)** can be a rewarding and challenging path for individuals interested in pursuing a career in accounting, finance, or management. A CMA is a globally recognized professional designation that signifies expertise in financial planning, analysis, control, and decision support.

5 Career Options in Cosmetology (Beauty Industry)

Beauty often charms the soul. Thus, from time immemorial, humans have sought to look beautiful by various means, from makeup, hairstyle to eye-catching attire. However, moving a step further, the desire to look beautiful has moved a step further. These days the industry is flourishing with experts that also make you 'feel beautiful' in your skin because technology has made many things possible. Checkout some out-of-the-box careers in this industry if you have considerable interest in this field.

1. **Skincare Specialist:** Beautiful skin is always a reflection of good health. Good skin also drives confidence. Thus, the job of a skincare specialist or an aesthetician is to enhance the appearance of an individual. They generally guide individuals

on how to reduce blemishes, improving their skin health, anti-aging procedures, etc. Aestheticians can find work in spas, hospitals, or private salons.
2. **Massage Therapist:** A massage not only enhances your external appearance, but it also detoxifies the body of negativity and relieves pains in specific parts, and, thus, relieves stress. This automatically leads to a glow on your face. The massage therapist uses his hands to relieve muscles and targets trigger points. There are various specializations in this like acupressure, sports massage, etc.
3. **Electrologist:** Electrology is the technique of hair removal through electrical epilation. Bodily hair is one irritant for women because it involves a tedious process of removal almost every month. Thus, this has become a flourishing industry as it offers a permanent solution to this problem. Currently, it is available in few colleges in Kerala, Uttar Pradesh, and Maharashtra.
4. **Aromatherapist:** Aromatherapy is using aroma from various extracts like barks, stems, flower oils to stimulate the body. It is believed that this has a beneficial effect on both the mind and body. These oils are inhaled and absorbed by the body and circulated into the bloodstream, which naturally soothes the body.
5. **Film and Theater Hair Specialist:** Hairstyles display one's personality, and this is why the right hairstyle in a performance is one of the most important parts of the theater or film industry. Hairstylist needs to be creative and experimenting to meet the demands of the performance.

6 Careers in Archaeology

A career in BA Archaeology can lead to various job opportunities in both public and private sectors. Some of the popular job profiles in this field are:

1. **Archaeologist:** An archaeologist is responsible for researching and excavating archaeological sites, analyzing artifacts and fossils, and interpreting them to gain insights into ancient cultures and societies.
2. **Heritage Manager:** A heritage manager is responsible for the preservation and maintenance of historical sites, monuments, and buildings. They oversee the development of exhibits, organize educational programs and workshops, and ensure that these sites are accessible to the public.
3. **Curator:** A curator is responsible for managing and maintaining collections of artifacts and specimens in museums, art galleries, and other cultural institutions. They research and identify items, acquire new pieces, organize exhibits and displays, and oversee conservation and preservation efforts.
4. **Historian:** Historians research and analyze historical events, figures, and societies, and create written and oral histories. They work in museums, archives, research centers, and educational institutions, and may specialize in different eras or regions.
5. **Academician:** With a degree in Archaeology, one can also pursue a career in academia as a professor or researcher. They can teach at universities and colleges, conduct research in various fields, and publish scholarly works in journals and books.
6. **Tour Guide:** With a deep understanding of history and culture, archaeologists can also work as tour guides in historical sites and museums. They lead groups of tourists and provide insights and information about the sites they are visiting.

Overall, a career in Archaeology can offer exciting opportunities to work with ancient artifacts, explore different cultures, and contribute to the preservation and promotion of heritage sites and monuments.

31 Upcoming Careers for future

Gone are the days when people used to work as switchboard operators, typists, or elevator operators. With the advent of technology, many traditional jobs have become obsolete. However, not all hope is lost. There are still plenty of jobs that are in demand and have a promising future. So, let's take a look at some of the hottest future careers across various industries and job fields.

1. **Nurse Practitioners:** Nurse practitioners are advanced practice registered nurses who provide primary and specialty healthcare services. They can diagnose and treat medical conditions, prescribe medications, and perform various medical procedures.
2. **Solar Photovoltaic Installers:** Solar photovoltaic installers are responsible for installing and maintaining solar panel systems on residential and commercial buildings. They work with various tools and equipment to ensure that solar panels are installed correctly and safely.
3. **Statisticians:** Statisticians are responsible for collecting, analyzing, and interpreting data to help organizations make informed decisions. They work in various industries, including healthcare, finance, and government.
4. **Physical Therapist Assistants:** Physical therapist assistants work with physical therapists to provide rehabilitation services to patients with physical injuries or illnesses. They help patients perform exercises and use various techniques to reduce pain and improve mobility.
5. **Information Security Analysts:** Information security analysts are responsible for protecting computer networks and systems from cyberattacks. They analyze data, identify potential security risks, and develop strategies to prevent security breaches.

6. **Animal Trainers:** Animal trainers are responsible for teaching animals to obey commands and perform specific behaviors. They may work with animals in various settings such as zoos, aquariums, circuses, and theme parks. In the future, animal trainers will continue to be in demand as the demand for animal-based entertainment and education increases. Animal trainers will also play a crucial role in the conservation and preservation of endangered species. They will work closely with scientists and veterinarians to develop training programs that will help animals adapt to new environments and improve their chances of survival in the wild.
7. **Nanotechnologist:** Nanotechnologists work with materials at the atomic and molecular level to create new products and technologies. In the future, nanotechnology will play a crucial role in many industries such as medicine, energy, and electronics. Nanotechnologists will be responsible for developing new materials and devices that will help solve problems such as pollution, energy shortages, and disease. They will also work on improving existing technologies such as computer chips, solar cells, and batteries.
8. **Pharmaviglence:** Pharmaviglence professionals monitor and analyze the safety and efficacy of drugs and medical devices. In the future, the demand for pharmaviglence professionals will increase as new drugs and devices are developed and brought to market. They will be responsible for ensuring that these products are safe and effective and do not cause any harm to patients. They will work closely with healthcare professionals, regulatory agencies, and pharmaceutical companies to ensure that patients receive the best possible care.
9. **Cyber Security:** Cybersecurity professionals protect computer systems and networks from cyber attacks and other security breaches. In the future, the demand for

cybersecurity professionals will continue to increase as more companies and organizations rely on technology to store sensitive information. Cybersecurity professionals will be responsible for developing and implementing security measures to prevent cyber attacks and protect against data breaches. They will also work on improving existing security measures and developing new technologies to stay ahead of cyber criminals.

10. **Embryology:** Embryologists study the development of embryos and the reproductive system. In the future, embryology will play a crucial role in many fields such as assisted reproductive technology, genetic engineering, and regenerative medicine. Embryologists will be responsible for developing new techniques to help infertile couples conceive, preventing genetic diseases, and growing replacement organs from stem cells.

11. **Computer Numerically Controlled Tool Programmers:** Computer numerically controlled tool programmers create programs that control the movements of machines such as lathes, mills, and routers. In the future, the demand for CNC tool programmers will continue to increase as more manufacturing processes become automated. CNC tool programmers will be responsible for developing programs that can produce parts with high precision and accuracy. They will also work on improving existing programs and developing new techniques to increase productivity and efficiency.

12. **Phlebotomists:** Phlebotomists are healthcare professionals who specialize in drawing blood from patients for medical testing, transfusions, donations, or research purposes. They typically work in hospitals, clinics, blood donation centers, or laboratories.Phlebotomists may have a variety of career paths available to them. They can advance their education and training to become medical laboratory technicians,

who perform a wider range of laboratory tests on patient samples, or medical laboratory technologists, who oversee laboratory operations and analyze more complex test results. Some phlebotomists may also choose to become nurse practitioners, physician assistants, or physicians with further education and training.

13. **Software Developers:** Software developers are responsible for designing, developing, testing, and maintaining computer software programs. They work in a variety of industries, such as technology, finance, healthcare, and entertainment. As technology continues to evolve, there will be a growing demand for software developers who specialize in areas such as artificial intelligence, cybersecurity, and cloud computing. Some software developers may choose to become software architects or project managers, who oversee the development process and ensure that projects are completed on time and within budget. Others may become technical writers or trainers, who create user manuals and training materials to help users learn how to use software programs.

14. **Software Quality Assurance Analysts And Testers:** Software quality assurance analysts and testers are responsible for ensuring that software programs are working properly and meeting quality standards. They typically test software for bugs, defects, and usability issues, and work with software developers to fix any problems they find. As more companies rely on software to conduct their business, the demand for software quality assurance analysts and testers is expected to grow. Some software quality assurance analysts and testers may choose to specialize in areas such as security testing, performance testing, or automation testing. They may also become quality assurance managers or directors, who oversee the testing process and ensure that software programs are meeting quality standards.

15. **Genetic Counsellors:** Genetic counsellors help individuals and families understand the genetic risks of certain diseases and conditions. In the future, the demand for genetic counsellors will increase as genetic testing becomes more common and accessible. Genetic counsellors will be responsible for providing information and support to individuals and families who are at risk of genetic disorders. They will also work with healthcare professionals to develop personalized treatment plans based on genetic information
16. **Home Health And Personal Care Aides:** Home health and personal care aides provide personal care services to elderly or disabled individuals in their homes. They help patients with daily living activities, such as bathing, dressing, and eating.
17. **Medical And Health Services Managers:** Medical and health services managers are responsible for managing healthcare facilities, such as hospitals and clinics. They ensure that healthcare services are delivered efficiently and effectively.
18. **Data Scientists And Mathematical Science Occupations, All Other:** Data scientists and mathematical science professionals work with data to identify trends, develop models, and make predictions. They work in various industries, including healthcare, finance, and technology.
19. **Physician Assistants:** Physician assistants work under the supervision of physicians to provide medical care to patients. They can diagnose and treat medical conditions, prescribe medications, and perform medical procedures.
20. **Epidemiologists:** Epidemiologists study the patterns and causes of diseases and injuries in human populations. They use various research methods to identify potential health risks and develop strategies to prevent the spread of diseases.
21. **Logisticians:** Logisticians are responsible for managing the supply chain process, from acquiring raw materials to

delivering finished products to customers. They ensure that products are delivered efficiently and cost-effectively.

22. **Speech-Language Pathologists:** Speech-language pathologists work with patients who have communication and swallowing disorders. They assess patients' communication abilities and develop treatment plans to help them improve their speech and language skills.

23. **Animal Trainers:** Animal trainers train animals for various purposes, such as entertainment, protection, and research. They use various training methods to teach animals specific behaviors and skills.

24. **Operations Research Analysts:** Operations research analysts are professionals who use mathematical and analytical techniques to solve complex problems and make better decisions. They analyze data and information to identify patterns and trends, and then use this information to develop models and simulations that can help organizations optimize their processes, reduce costs, and improve efficiency. The careers for operations research analysts can be found in a variety of industries, including healthcare, finance, logistics, and manufacturing.

25. **Forest Fire Inspectors And Prevention Specialists:** Forest fire inspectors and prevention specialists are professionals who work to prevent and manage wildfires in forested areas. They inspect forested areas to identify potential hazards, such as dry brush or dead trees, and then develop and implement plans to mitigate those risks. Forest fire inspectors and prevention specialists typically work for government agencies, such as the U.S. Forest Service.

26. **Interpreters And Translators:** Interpreters and translators are professionals who help individuals and organizations communicate across language barriers. They may work in a variety of settings, including hospitals, courtrooms, and businesses, and must be fluent in multiple languages.

Interpreters and translators may specialize in specific industries or fields, such as medical or legal translation.
27. **Sports Trainers:** Sportstrainers are healthcare professionals who work with athletes and other physically active individuals to prevent and treat injuries. They may provide first aid, rehabilitation services, or injury prevention programs, and may work in a variety of settings, including schools, universities, or sports medicine clinics.
28. **Respiratory Therapists:** Respiratory therapists are healthcare professionals who help patients with breathing and lung-related problems. They may work with patients of all ages, from premature infants to elderly adults, and provide treatments such as oxygen therapy or mechanical ventilation. Respiratory therapists may work in hospitals, clinics, or home healthcare settings.
29. **Mental Health Counselors:** Mental health counselors are professionals who work with individuals who have addiction or mental health issues. They may provide counseling services, develop treatment plans, and work with other healthcare professionals to provide comprehensive care. Mental health counselors may work in a variety of settings, including hospitals, clinics, or private practices.
30. **Food Preparation And Serving Related Workers,:** Food preparation and serving related workers, all other, is a broad category of professionals who work in the food service industry. This may include food service managers, chefs, and food preparation workers, among others. These professionals typically work in restaurants, hotels, or other food service establishments.

7 Career Options For Those Who Love Insurance

1. **Actuary:** An actuary is a trained statistician with expertise in evaluating risks. They play an essential role in deciding the

terms and conditions for insurance policies. They are needed for forecasting future payouts and pension fund management.
2. **Insurance Appraiser:** Insurance appraisers are experts who value certain types of property. They also provide expert advice to insurance claim adjusters. They are an important part of the insurance firms.
3. **Insurance Claim Adjusters:** Insurance claim adjusters are given a vital task to determine whether the claim made by a party regarding loss is justified under an insurance policy and in what amount.
4. **Insurance Claims Examiner:** Similar to Insurance claims adjusters in some parts, these examiners are the experts in the case of health and life insurance. But in the case of property and casualty insurance, the task is often given to a senior adjuster.
5. **Insurance Investigators:** They are private detectives in the insurance sector. They assist insurance claims adjusters and examiners in case of suspected fraud, especially if the claim is large.
6. **Insurance Sales Agent:** Insurance sales agents are given the task of making insurance available to the masses. In some cases, they may also act as financial planners. The agents with an insurance firm are referred to as "captive agents" while the ones working independently are "insurance brokers."
7. **Insurance Underwriters:** Insurance underwriters are the ones who analyze insurance applications and determine if they should be accepted or rejected. Most of the time, they take a back-office role but can also accompany the latter on sales calls.

5 Career choices for extroverts

For an extrovert, the world is a place where every new person or event is an opportunity to gain a unique experience. They never shy away from challenges and are open to changes. Their most apparent quality is their willingness to interact with people. So if you are an extrovert, these five career options are best suited for you.

1. **Lawyer:** Being a lawyer means that you will have to deal with different kinds of people and situations. Since extroverts are open to social interactions and have a knack for effectively handling unexpected situations, they often make good lawyers.
2. **Mediator:** When any legal dispute, like a property dispute, arises, a mediator often resolves the issue between the two warring parties outside the courtroom. A mediator has the rare skill of persuasion and effectively communicates his viewpoint so that the dispute is resolved and an agreement is reached without having to take the matter to court.
3. **Public Relations:** Public Relations is an area in media and communication, and a public relations specialist can work for any organization. Their work is to maintain the public image of the organization. They have to interact with print and broadcast media to ensure favorable coverage. To become a public relations specialist, one should have excellent interpersonal skills, which, more often than not, an extrovert possesses.
4. **Event Planner:** Organizing an event, whether a party or a professional conference of a particular organization or government department, the event planner has to manage and plan everything from the venue, the schedule of the event to the transportation and handling of other key areas involved. Being an extrovert gives one an edge over introverts because they are often good at managing, communicating, and guiding people working under them.
5. **Journalist:** The job of a journalist is to interact with people and find the relevant news. A journalist often has to travel and seek

out news. Since extroverts are always open to new experiences, unlike introverts, they often make good journalists.

5 Career Options For Introverts

Introverts have always been a shy lot and are often criticized for their reluctance to engage with people. However, this very quality can become its strength. Various job options demand qualities like calmness, solitariness, and perseverance.

1. **Writer:** A writer always prefers his imaginative world to the real one. This is one job that is the most solitary. It best suits those who have writing as their forte and prefer working alone. So if you are an introvert who likes to write, then this is the perfect option to go for. However, you need to be patient before hard work starts yielding results.
2. **Artist:** Just like writing, any piece of art expresses the feelings of the artist. Introverts like to express their emotions in indirect ways, and art is one of the media to express these emotions. This is a large field as there is a whole range of options available, for example, painters, sculpturist, dancers, singers, etc.
3. **Program Developer:** A programmer spends hours alone, working on his software or program. So this is one of the jobs which require one to sit and work on your project. Since introverts are calm and patient by nature, this tends to be a suitable option. To become a software developer, you need to have a sound knowledge of computers and programming.
4. **Information And Technology Professional:** IT professions have technical knowledge of computers and work in areas concerning networking, database administration, engineering, and e-commerce. This field requires working mostly with computers and related areas.
5. **Scientist:** This is another field that requires a lot of time researching and experimenting. Since introverts have the

unique ability to enjoy their own company and avoid human company for days, they can take up this as a career option. However, to become a scientist, one needs to be analytical, experimental, and can think out of the box.

8 Careers in advertising and marketing

There are many career options available in the field of advertising and marketing. Here are some of the most popular ones:

1. **Advertising Manager:** Advertising managers are responsible for creating and implementing advertising campaigns for their clients or their own company. They manage teams of creative professionals, media planners and buyers, and other personnel to produce ads that meet the client's marketing goals and objectives.
2. **Market Research Analyst:** Market research analysts study market conditions to determine the potential sales of a product or service. They help companies understand what people want, who will buy their products, and at what price. This information is used to create marketing campaigns and develop new products.
3. **Digital Marketing Specialist:** Digital marketing specialists develop and implement online marketing strategies. They use social media, email, and other digital channels to reach potential customers and drive sales. They also analyze data to determine the effectiveness of their campaigns and adjust their strategies accordingly.
4. **Public Relations Specialist:** Public relations specialists help companies build and maintain a positive image. They write press releases, create media kits, and develop strategies to promote a company's products or services. They also work to minimize the impact of negative publicity.
5. **Brand Manager:** Brand managers are responsible for building and maintaining a company's brand image. They work with

advertising and marketing teams to develop campaigns that reinforce the brand's values and messaging. They also manage the company's online reputation and social media presence.
6. **Media Planner/Buyer:** Media planners and buyers are responsible for identifying the most effective media channels for a company's advertising campaigns. They negotiate rates and placement for print, radio, TV, and online ads, and analyze data to determine the success of their campaigns.
7. **Copywriter:** Copywriters create the text for ads and other marketing materials. They write headlines, taglines, and body copy that engage customers and drive sales. They also work with art directors and designers to create a cohesive campaign message.
8. **Account Executive:** Account executives are the main point of contact between an advertising agency and its clients. They work to understand the client's marketing objectives and ensure that their needs are met by the agency. They also manage the creative team and other agency personnel to ensure that campaigns are delivered on time and on budget.

5 Career Options for Those Who Are Witty

We recently conducted a session for some students, which turned out to be engaging and a lot of fun. At the end of the session, we were forced to agree that kids can teach us a lot of things and act as a catalyst to our imagination and curiosity. The frontbenchers and toppers get their fair share of praises, but the backbenchers are no less, so never think that they are good for nothing. With their sharp wit that hits bang on and an interesting one-liner that can leave you in splits, they can amaze all and force us to think more. Here is a list of 5 career options that suit them best.

1. **Presenters:** A presenter at an event requires quick wit, sharp humor and has to be sociable and an extrovert. With all these

qualities naturally present in people who love to blow us away while enjoying a lazy day, this opportunity makes it an easy option.
2. **Critics:** Highly revered in the industries, critics are hard to please. They'll analyze things and situations keenly and then pass a verdict that can create or break all. Our commentators, too, are hard nuts to crack, and their feedback is considered valuable enough because they analyze everything rather than take it for face value.
3. **Advertising:** These backbenchers come up with such eye-catching lines that it's difficult to miss them. This is what the advertising industry demands – creativity, innovation, and out-of-the-box thinking.
4. **RJ/VJ:** With an excellent command over their words and an aim to entertain, our most loved chatterboxes have a reason to smile. You can use your wit to enthrall people by being a radio or video jockey.
5. **Comedian:** It is a difficult task for anyone to make others laugh without offending them. As a comedian, you can take a dig at anyone – throw your comments at the audience or punch out a satire – without being executed. After all, they are the authorized mirror of and to the society. Plus, it's a lucrative career choice these days.

5 Career Options for Night Owls

As we grow up, our routine sometimes tends to shift to suit to night time. When the whole world sleeps, we wake up. The silence of the night helps us concentrate better. And what better than getting to earn during these hours? Check out these five career choices for night owls.

1. **Radio Jockey:** Radio Jockeys do a noble job of keeping the distressed people happy at night hours. They spread music, liveliness, and happiness in the air.

2. **Disc Jockey:** Like RJs, they can turn any spot into a party place. With adrenaline rising music and over-enthusiastic attitude, they can turn a dull night into a crazy one.
3. **Call Center Executives:** India is a hub of call centers. With many multinationals outsourcing their work, Indian call center executives are attracting them with their skills. Our nightcrawlers can work for multinationals and earn more than their day shift counterparts.
4. **Firefighters:** Firefighters have to be ready at all times. They are much in demand at night because that's the time tragedy can strike unaware. For the night owls, this provides them an opportunity to be heroes in the true sense.
5. **Taxi Drivers:** If you love to drive and be left alone at night, there is no reason to not roam around the street, helping passengers reach their desired destinations. You do what you love and also earn some extra bucks.

5 Career Options for People Who are Good Listeners

Speaking is one of the most common ways of communication, and excellent communication cannot take place unless the receiver understands the information accurately. In other words, good listening skill is one of the factors influencing effective communication. A good listener will always appreciate the underlying meaning of the conveyed information and also pay attention to non-verbal and para-verbal cues. Some jobs concerning this skill might seem attractive to some people.

1. **Counselors:** A counselor has to hear the problems of people, understand their situation, and propose a solution to it. They cater to the different needs of different people, who suffer from various issues. Counselors are present in every organization, whether it's a school, an office, or an NGO. Career counselors, de-addiction counselors, marriage counselors, etc. are some examples.

2. **Translators:** Excellent listening skill is a mandatory requirement in this field because translators have to listen and understand what is said in one language and accurately translate it into another language in such a way that the meaning and essence is not lost.
3. **Salesperson:** The first task of the salesperson is to understand and identify what the customer seeks and wants. They have to pinpoint the interests of the customer and, thus, adapt their ways according to the needs. A good salesperson will always listen to the consumer and identify the target area.
4. **Civil Mediators:** Some issues like property, marriage, workplace-related disputes are common and need to be resolved outside the court. Civil mediators try to resolve a conflict between two disputing parties. Thus, excellent listening skills give an upper hand to mediators.
5. **Any Leadership Position:** A leader, be it a CEO, manager, or teacher, needs to have the unique quality of listening to other's points of view and understanding the people working under them. A good leader always listens more and speaks only when required.

8 Careers in language &literature

Studying language and literature can have a wide range of career and personal benefits. Here are some of the scopes of studying language and literature:

1. **Teaching:** One of the most common career paths for language and literature graduates is to become a teacher. You can teach at schools, colleges, or universities.
2. **Writing and Editing:** A degree in language and literature can help you develop strong writing and editing skills, which can be applied to a variety of fields. You can work as a content writer, journalist, copy editor, or technical writer.

3. **Translation and Interpretation:** If you have a strong proficiency in multiple languages, you can work as a translator or interpreter in government agencies, businesses, or NGOs.
4. **Publishing:** With a degree in language and literature, you can work in the publishing industry as a literary agent, editor, or marketer.
5. **Research:** A language and literature degree can prepare you for advanced research in fields such as linguistics, literary theory, or cultural studies.
6. **Civil Services:** Proficiency in language and literature is often an asset for jobs in government services, particularly for positions that require excellent communication skills.
7. **International Business:** Multinational corporations often prefer to hire individuals who have a strong proficiency in a foreign language, as it enables them to work effectively with global teams and clients.
8. **Personal Growth:** Studying language and literature can broaden your horizons and provide you with a deeper understanding of different cultures, histories, and perspectives.

Overall, a degree in language and literature can lead to a diverse range of career opportunities, while also providing you with a valuable set of transferable skills.

5 Career Options for Those Who Love To Write

Many amongst us passionate about reading and writing. We love to scribble down every small detail and are always looking for opportunities to write a bestseller. But what if we could earn a living doing what we love the most? Yes, many career options revolve around writing. Here's a list of 5 career options to look out for if you have a way with the words and love to pen down your thoughts.

1. **Content Developers:** One of the fastest emerging options available, content developers are assigned the task of creating eye-catching content for firms that conveys their vision and work to the target audience. With the technological advancements, people want crisp and notable content that does not take pages to explain.
2. **Author:** If you're the one who lives in a fantastical world and wants to narrate your story, then you can be an author. All you need is a penchant for writing, a-way with the words, and a strong imagination.
3. **Journalists:** A journalist is one who collects and writes about any relevant information that needs to be told to the world. For being a journalist, you need to be an active person with a knack for playing with words. And journalism is not just limited to newsletters but also various other fields. Ever heard of sports journalists or agricultural journalists?
4. **Blogger:** Everything in today's world is based on technology. With blogs and websites popping up like popcorns, the role of bloggers has spurted. It is now seen as a vital part of marketing.
5. **Proofreader:** This career may not seem glamorous, but it is a steady option. Proofreaders are required to correct grammatical mistakes in a literary draft without changing the author's content to make it fit for publishing.

10 Career Options for Those Who Are Born Artists

1. **Street Artists:** Street artists are those who love to puff life into dilapidated walls or places and bring them to the spotlight again with their artwork. This emerging art form is in so much craze that a full 2 ½ month festival is dedicated to it where local and international participants at various stages.
2. **Cartoonist:** Cartoonists are those who bring inanimate objects to life. In simple terms, he is a visual expert who

draws cartoons. But life would not have been comfortable and colorful had the cartoons not been made.
3. **Book Illustrator:** Most of us who do not read voluntarily pick up texts only to browse through it quickly. And what we look for is impressive illustrations, which not only brings colors into a drab text but also summarizes the plot for us.
4. **Jewelry Designer:** Diamonds are a girl's best friend, and so is any other jewelry. And now, it's also a favorite of men who love to show off some gold. But those gorgeous pieces of jewelry that dazzle people is the hard work and analysis of jewelry designers.
5. **Painters:** One usually looks at artists like painters, but it is not easy to describe a painter. Their art is subjective and ranges from graphics, stencils to geometrical shapes, and others.
6. **Animator:** An animator is a person who brings to life the works of a cartoonist to create animation.
7. **Drafter:** A drafter is someone who uses software to convert the designs of engineers and architects into technical drawings and plans.
8. **Graphic Designer:** A graphic designer is a professional person who assembles together images, typography, and motion pictures to create a piece of design.
9. **Tattoo Artist:** Tattoo artists are in high demand at present times. So, if you are the one who is fascinated by body art, you should try being a tattoo artist.
10. **Mehndi Artists:** India, with its numerous festivals where applying mehndi on hands, is a must, is witnessing tremendous growth in the industry. With people earning above Rs. 5000 in a single event, it is a lucrative business.

6 career options if you love music

Music always stirs a part of our souls, and it is this inherent quality that makes us fall for music at some time or the other. Though everyone isn't gifted with a melodious voice to become a singer, there are other career options to tread if you think music is your passion.

1. **Music Composer-** A musical performance is never complete without good background music, which is harmonious. A composer creates and directs music for a song, theatre, or other media. So if you have the right ear for music and are creatively inclined, then this is a perfect career option for you. As a composer, you should always know how to read music notation.
2. **Music Teacher-** A music teacher is one who gives singing lessons and teaches musical instruments. These days schools, independent institutions hire music teachers to teach choirs, bands. Though one can always provide private music tuitions.
3. **Disc Jockey-** A DJ plays and mixes songs for live performances like parties or broadcasts on the radio or televisions. The DJ picks the type of music genre that best suits the mood of the audience and prepares a playlist. To become a DJ, you need to be passionate and a bit experimental.
4. **Studio Musician-** Studio musicians are performers who play instruments at the time of recordings or live performances. If you are good at playing any instruments, then you can be a part of the musical compositions in any part of the media industry.
5. **Music Journalist/Critic-** A music critic decides and judges what defines good music. For example, after hearing a piece of work, a music critic has to make a commentary, evaluate, and critically analyze the composition. To become a music journalist, you need to have a sound knowledge of music and its workings.

6. **Music Therapist-** Music is not just an art but also an effective way to soothe the nerves. Music therapy is a medical profession, and you need to be good at understanding the mental state of patients. A music therapist understands the needs of his patient, whether psychological or physical, and provides appropriate music, which helps in healing.

5 Career Options for Movie Buffs

As Indians, we've grown up watching movies. They have taught us a lot, be it "about loving your family" or love or friendship. With the release of any film, we book our tickets and plan our day out. What if being a movie buff could pay you well? These are some of the career options a diehard movie fan can look forward to.

1. **Movie Reviewer:** Being a movie reviewer is the perfect task for a movie buff because you get paid to watch a movie and pass your judgment. Now, who wouldn't want such a lifestyle?
2. **Scriptwriter:** A scriptwriter is responsible for penning down meaningful dialogues for the movies. This job allows for a lot of creativity. The movie's business relies a lot on its writers who shape the director's dream to present it on the screen.
3. **Actor/Actress:** The lead stars of the show grab a lot of attention when a movie hits the theatres every Friday morning. If you prefer to work in front of the camera and be the center of attraction, you can be an actor or actress.
4. **Editor:** With a strong sense of what's in and required for a particular scene, the editor has a lot of power and can even challenge the director's work. And guess what? You'll be paid for turning the director mad, and if your decisions prove to be beneficial, you might be a sought-after editor.
5. **Runner:** Though it is not a lucrative opportunity because, as the name suggests, you just have to run around and work with

the departments. You could also be called to fill in any vacant position, so you get the best of all worlds.

5 Career Options for Those Who Love To Eat

Being 21st-century youth, there are two things we are never shy of – sleeping and eating. We live on food, and we live for food. We are people with golden hearts who take the meaning of 'AtithiDevoBhavah' too seriously and choke our relatives with numerous plates of irresistibly mouthwatering dishes neatly kept on the table. But what if our fetish for food could help us earn a few bucks? My bad, not a few but a lot of bucks. So, here are five career options that revolve around food and drinks. (And, these career options only include eating and drinking; no other pressure.)

1. **Tea Taster:** A tea taster is held in high regard because it is up to him to taste and grade different varieties of tea based on quality. He decides the rate of the tea, which can, at times, be as high as Rs. 1.12 lakh per kilogram.
2. **Sommelier:** He's an expert on wine and specializes in wine service and wine-food pairing. A sommelier is a reputed and knowledgeable person in the food and beverage industry, and his opinion is of the utmost importance when it comes to wine.
3. **Chocolate Taster:** What can be better to be surrounded by chocolates all day and get to eat all varieties of chocolates? Well, if this is your fantasy world, then you can sign up for this career.
4. **Food Critic:** One person that can disarm people in a restaurant and demands high respect is a food critic. He is such a dreaded person that everyone wants to please them. On the other hand, a food critic gets to munch on different dishes from around the world and pass his judgment that can make or break a restaurant's reputation.

5. **Culinary Tour Guide:** If you love the hidden culinary world in your city and want to explore it, then this is the career option for you. You get to walk around the city, searching for different cuisines and what gets into making them and try out some of the best.
PS. Some places might even give you a sneak peek into their kitchens and serve you their offerings.

7 Career Options for Those Who Love To Travel

Many of us love to travel. One thing that we hate the most is stagnation, and traveling is an exercise that reminds us of movement and growth. So, come weekends or holidays, we pack our bag packs and head towards different directions in search of adventure and fun. But what if traveling could be your career and you could earn a handsome salary by traveling and covering places? Here's a list of some career options for those who love to travel.

1. **Travel Tour Guide:** India is a nation with a rich cultural history. You'll find a monument or a place with a new account at every turn. Many tourists, national or international, flock in to see these and often require amiable and knowledgeable tour guides who can lead them through city sights.
2. **Travel Blogger:** If you love to travel and write, then this career option is best suited for you. It combines two of the most relaxing and adventurous things – traveling and writing. Many websites, today, are dedicated to providing 360-degree information to people who wish to visit those places.
3. **International Aid Worker:** If you want to travel for a cause that can bring about meaningful change in people's lives, you can be an international aid worker. You will get to visit countries that require aid to recover from any natural or human-made calamity.

4. **Destination Wedding Photographer:** This profession is best suited for those who love to travel and capture the scenic beauty of the place. Being a destination wedding photographer allows you to document the big day of the couple and enjoy the additional benefits of your work.
5. **Commercial Pilots:** If you love to give wings to your dreams, then you can be a commercial pilot. Traveling to different destinations and being able to enjoy the view from the front row makes the career option attractive. The only difficulty that they encounter is jet lags that can affect them in a meaningful manner.
6. **WWOOF:** As a volunteer with World Wide Opportunities on Organic Farms, or Willing Workers on Organic Farms (WWOOF) you get an opportunity to select a nation of your own choice, stay with the host (from the other country) and help them in organic farming in exchange for accommodation and food.
7. **Travel Show Host:** What if you score a travel show deal? You get paid to have fun, enjoy and travel for free. Being a travel show host buys you comfort that many dreams of so if you love to chatter and have a charismatic personality with a flair for traveling, join in.

5 Career Options for Those Who Love Clothing

A sign of love for clothing is an irresistible urge to check out people's clothes and the latest trends. People harboring this love always inspect the quality of the cloth before buying something new because they have an exquisite sense of understanding of the texture and have a keen eye for the material. There are many career options for people who love playing with the cloth.

1. **Fashion Designer:** This is the most sought after career in this area. A fashion designer needs to not only have the knowledge

of textile but also trending styles and a very creative bent of mind to create original pieces of apparel. As a designer, you can start your label or supply clothing to other well-established brands.

2. **Carpet Designer:** Who said clothes are the only product a person can design. A carpet designer has to do the same thing for carpets that decorate our homes and office. And that is not such an easy task. This job also requires high levels of creativity and innovation. Carpet designers often use computer software to create designs.

3. **Interior Designer:** Interior designing is a vast field but involves a sufficient amount of knowledge of textiles. It includes planning and creating aesthetically appealing decors and interiors. What type of curtains should be used, the type of cushion covers and bedsheets, carpets that will make the room look complete, is one of the jobs of the interior decorator.

4. **Clothing Store Manager:** Who said that a career in clothing only involves working in the production cycle? A clothing store manager is the head of a retail store and manages all its functions. This is the end cycle where the finished products are sold to the consumers.

5. **Clothing Manufacturing Engineer:** This is a technical job. A piece of cloth is manufactured in a factory, and the position of the manufacturing engineer is to assemble the machines so that they work properly.

7 Career Options For People Who Love Fitness

Fitness is something that some people ignore, and some people worship. However, if you are one of the few people who are not just passionate about keeping your own body healthy but also want to help others to remain fit, then the following career options are just right for you.

1. **Fitness Trainer:** A fitness trainer works in a gym or any other health center and guides the work regime of people according to their needs. He/she has to inspire people so that they exercise regularly and remain fit.
2. **Recreation Worker:** They are responsible for organizing and leading activities that involve sports and other types of outdoor leisure activities for volunteer agencies or in camps, parks, etc.
3. **Dietician:** Food is the most important thing that determines a person's health. So, to remain healthy, we need to have a balanced diet according to specific needs. A dietician determines a food chart that a person should follow to suit his/her particular needs, which also gives sufficient nutrition.
4. **Coach:** If you bear a passion for any specific sports and are good at it, then you can train and guide youngsters who are aiming to make a career in that sport. This job can also be done part-time and is often very satisfying.
5. **Yoga Coach:** Yoga has become one of the most popular ways to remain fit because it heals not only the body but also the soul. To become a yoga teacher, one needs to get a certification to teach yoga. After that, one can open his/her institute for yoga or yoga studio or work as a personal trainer.
6. **Physical Therapist:** Physical therapy involves stimulating the muscles to improve movement in limbs and joints. After an injury, surgery, or illness, a physical therapist uses various techniques and exercises to help patients recover.
7. **Massage Therapist:** Living in a stressful environment can often give people jitters, and so many people are opting for massages as a way to relieve their stress. A massage therapist helps people to relax according to their requirements. They also help people recover from injuries.

5 Career Options for Tech Savvy People

Technology has become an essential part of our lives, so people who can handle and have a good knowledge of technology will find great opportunities that are booming in this sector.

1. **Computer Programmer:** A computer programmer has to develop computer applications and software. He not only has to code the software but also check its efficiency and user-friendliness. To become a programmer, one has to know some of the primary computer languages like C++, C#, Java, Python, Lisp, etc.
2. **Game Designer:** Video games are the new craze among the young these days. Therefore, game designers have a considerable scope. They have to design characters, create situations and puzzles that will form the structure of the game. Knowledge of animation and programming is necessary for this field.
3. **UX/UI Designer:** A User Interface (UI) designer has to design interactive interfaces for machines and software, which range from mobile applications, electronic devices, computers, etc. As a User Experience (UX) designer, one has to ensure that the interaction between user and product is maximized, and the interfaces are user-friendly.
4. **Web Developer:** Websites are designed by programmers and designers who code and develop how a website will look and function when used by a user.
5. **Security Analyst:** Since almost all of the crucial data related to a company is stored on computers, there is a risk of sensitive information falling into the wrong hands. Security analysts are responsible for building the security system in such a way that prevents hackers from stealing crucial information. They also have to upgrade the network security system regularly.

5 Off-beat Career Options In Arrangement And Display

When an everyday thing is presented appealingly, then even the most mundane thing becomes extraordinary and likable. Therefore, the role of the artful exhibition becomes of immense importance for something that is marketable.

1. **Food Stylist:** Also called food photography, food styling is one of the evolving career options these days as food photography plays a vital role in marketing and commercialization (for magazines, menus, cookbooks, and newspaper) of food products. The function of the food photographer is to make the food look desirable. Thus, one needs to have a good sense of arrangement and culinary knowledge.
2. **Floral Arranger:** Arranging flowers is an art in itself which involves passion, love, and an eye to harmony. A floral planner might be employed at weddings or events where an arrangement of flowers is required.
3. **Picture Framer:** A beautiful picture always requires an appropriate frame to complete it. Professional picture framers make and pick the best frames that might suit a painting or a photograph. Creativity and precision are important in this career.
4. **Museum Curator:** A curator is someone who manages the work of art, which also involves display, educating the public, and marketing of artwork.
5. **Exhibition Planner:** An exhibition planner has to organize and plan an exhibition. He/she has to oversee all the functions from how the venue of the exhibition should look to the itinerary of the event.

5 Career Options in Jewellery Industry

Imagine, how would life be without all those glittering ornaments and precious gems to adorn ourselves with? A woman's most treasured objects are her jewellery. So, if you were wondering about the career options available in this field, then read further for a short guide to the jewellery industry.

1. **Jewellery Designer:** To become a jewellery designer, you need to have excellent designing skills and a keen eye for intricacy and detail. There are specialized jewellery designing courses, and as a designer, you can work for an established firm or design under your name.
2. **Gem Expert:** Gemology is a science that involves working and studying natural and artificial gems. Gemologists work in labs and identify and work on gemstones and their quality and impurities.
3. **Jewellery Quality Assurance Technician:** A jewellery quality assurance technician has to work in labs to test and provide certification for the quality of jewellery.
4. **Jewellery Store Manager:** A degree in management is enough to become a manager in a jewellery store. However, a sound knowledge of jewelry will only add to your skills.
5. **Antique Jewellery Expert:** Jewellery worn by our ancestors but no longer in fashion makes them a fit object for a museum. As an antique jewelry expert, one has to study old jewellery, identify which period it belongs to, what kind of material was used. The cultural aspects of the region it belongs to.

15 Career Options for Nature Lovers

In today's technologically advanced world where everyone competes to get hold of the latest gadgets and immerse themselves in it, a few manage to be a part of the magnificence of the bright blue sky, lush green trees, and the melodious cooing of the birds. If you think you fit in very well to the second category and nature is your true calling, then you should try these career options, which will give you satisfaction and money.

1. **Photographer:** A photographer aims to capture the marvels through his lens and provides an opportunity for the world to be a part of nature's brilliance. They give you a sneak peek into the secret world of flora and fauna.
2. **Organic Farmer:** Though farming looks like a work of the past world, the trend of organic farming is catching up. For nature lovers, it is a boon as they get to nurture the plants themselves and enjoy the freshness, ripeness, and sweetness of their hard work.
3. **Park Rangers:** What would it be like to be surrounded by the natural beauties of the city and earn money by showing people around? Park Rangers are the guardians of the natural parks and assist park guests in exploring the area.
4. **Conservation Scientist:** Conservation scientists are armed people with a mission – to conserve and protect the environment. They work closely to understand the surroundings and identify the best ways to use natural resources judiciously.
5. **Botanist:** For those whose life revolves around plants so much so that they want to gather all the information about them, being a botanist is in the cards for you. Since this is a broad field, one can choose a specialization according to their preference like field botany for those who want to search for new plant species or medicinal botany to understand the medicinal properties of different plants.
6. **Agricultural Contractor:** Agriculture contractors provide services to farmers and others like staff, resources, and other facilities. Other things in an agricultural contactor's to-do list include harvesting, animal breeding, crop spraying, et cetera.
7. **Animal Technician:** As an animal technician, you would be responsible for the day-to-day needs of lab animals. One would be required to help scientists with experiments involving the animals.

8. **Assistance Dog Trainers and Instructors:** They are responsible for training dogs to help people who have physical disabilities, medical conditions, and hearing or sight difficulties.
9. **Dog Groomers:** Dog groomers play an essential part in the animal's life. They are not only responsible for keeping dogs' coats in good condition but also advise their owners on coat care, grooming, and diet.
10. **Grounds Person:** As a grounds person, your work is to maintain the gorgeously colored sports grounds and carry out timely maintenance. If you are a sports and nature lover, this could be the best thing to happen to you.
11. **Horse Riding Instructor:** As a horse-riding instructor, your work would be to instruct and guide the learners. You'll get to be with horses in the lush green grounds and also earn while training people.
12. **Horticultural Therapists:** Horticultural therapists make use of the technique of gardening to cure or improve their client's mental and physical health. So, if you love to spend quality time with the plants and use your knowledge to heal people, this is the career for you.
13. **Ornithologist:** Being an ornithologist allows you to work in a variety of roles involving the study of behavior, ecology, classification, and conservation of birds and their habitats.
14. **RSPCA Inspectors:** These crusaders investigate and help prevent cruelty to animals. If you love animals and want to make a difference in their lives, this job could be perfect for you.
15. **Tree Surgeon:** Ever heard of a tree surgeon? Also known as tree climbers or arborists, they are the ones who carry out all kinds of tree work, including planting, care, and maintenance, and tree hazard assessments.

6 career options for animal lovers

We share this wonderful world not just with our fellow human beings but also with a wide range of wildlife. If you love animals or have a concern for them, then you might find many professions that not only fetches a handsome salary but brings along great satisfaction. Helping and spending time with animals can prove to be a great experience. You just have to figure out which one suits you best.

1. **Veterinarian-** A veterinarian is an animal doctor. If you like helping an animal, then this might become one of the most fulfilling jobs.
2. **Zoologist-** Someone who studies animals, their behavior, diseases, and genetics is called a zoologist. She/he should have excellent scientific and reasoning skills, a love for animals, and a lot of stamina to work off-hours, which involves doing on-field research to gather information and study animals. There are various specializations in this area, like animal biology, wildlife conservation, animal psychology, etc.
3. **Marine Biologist-** Since a whole array of life exits in the oceans and seas, marine biologists study organisms in water like fishes, plants, algae, mammals, reptiles, and other microscopic life.
4. **Animal Trainer-** An animal and pet trainer works on teaching pets how to obey their masters and also on behavior correction.
5. **Wildlife Photographer-** Do you love the way a monkey holds its baby or a peacock spreading its beautiful plumage? If you feel a strong desire to capture these beautiful moments in your camera and make them immortal, then wildlife photography might be the right choice. To become a wildlife photographer, you need to be patient because it can take hours before you get the perfect shot. It also requires lots of traveling to remote areas and jungles.
6. **Animal Rights Activist-** The growing outcry for a ban on animal cruelty has led to the emergence of many animal rights

groups. They champion the causes of animals so that their present situations can be improved. To become an animal activist, one should be eloquent, dedicated, and express a strong belief in animals' right to a quality life.

10 Super Cool Career Options to Look Out For

1. **Food Stylist:** A food stylist is a person who arranges food to make it appear attractive for the advertisements. For the basics, you need to have a great visual concept, an understanding of what might appeal to the public, color sense, and presentation skills.
2. **Holiday Consultant:** A trained person in the travel and tourism industry who assists potential customers by providing them travel solutions for vacations, business, and holidays. A proper sales technique, a love for traveling, and an understanding of the market can help you grab an opportunity.
3. **Modeling:** For presentable young men and women who ooze a lot of confidence and whose body language says it all, modeling has always been an exciting career choice. Many of our stars started as models.
4. **News Reader:** News readers have a vital role in informing the nation about the latest happenings around the world. Knowledgeable, confident, presentable with excellent communication skills; they are the super-cool heroes of today.
5. **Photographers:** Patient, focused with an eye for scenic beauty photographers are needed to capture the marvels in every field.
6. **Photo Journalist:** A photojournalist creates stories through their photographs. It requires confidence, intuition, patience, compassion, and a bit of wanderlust to click things.

7. **Social Media Manager:** A Social Media Manager is responsible for the content and messages of an organization in the online social media platform. They need to be high multitaskers with eagerness to learn.
8. **UX Designer:** User Experience designer incorporates all aspects of user-focused design considerations, including information architecture, user testing, and visual design. With everything turning online, there's a great demand for UX designers.
9. **Dance Therapist:** Dance therapy involves the use of movements and dance to help cure the emotional and physical needs of the people.
10. **Personal Shopper:** What if you could get paid for shopping? Personal shoppers help you decide your look for an occasion, keeping in mind your style and help you shop. Now, who wouldn't love that?

10 OFFBEAT CAREER OPTIONS

1. **Veterinary Science and Animal Husbandry:** If all you can think of is about is animals, then this is the course for you. From studying animal physiology, nutrition, reproduction, and livestock management to animal diseases and meat hygiene and technology, you study it all.
2. **Sommelier:** He's an expert on wine and specializes in wine service and wine-food pairing. A sommelier is a reputed and knowledgeable person in the food and beverage industry, and his opinion is of the utmost importance when it comes to wine.
3. **Ocean Engineering:** If you wish to enjoy the best of both worlds of engineering and marine life, Ocean engineering provides you a rare chance. This field deals with research and development, design, testing, operation, and maintenance of marine structures and vehicles.

4. **Tea Taster:** A tea taster is held in high regard because it is up to him to taste and grade different varieties of tea based on quality. He decides the rate of the tea, which can, at times, be as high as Rs. 1.12 lakh per kilogram.
5. **Fashion Choreographer:** A fashion choreographer is one who directs the whole fashion show. From discussions with designers to understand their vision of directing the models on stage, they do it all.
6. **Archaeology:** A subset of Anthropology, Archaeology, tries to understand the history of humans by studying the material culture and environment data that has been left behind. All the stuff about mummies and unearthing old civilizations are included here.
7. **Unani Experts:** A traditional system of health maintenance and healing has its origins in Greece, Persia, and Arabia before the Mughals brought it to India. India has 40 Unani medical colleges where the subject is taught.
8. **Forensic Accounting:** Sherlock Holmes in the Commerce stream, they shoulder the responsibility of using their accounting skills to investigate cases of fraud.
9. **Occupational Therapist:** Occupational therapists make use of creative actives activities to heal patients suffering from mental or physical illness.
10. **Visual Merchandising:** A visual merchandiser creates and develops the floor plan and ensures that their goods are presented to the audience in a manner to best highlight their benefits.

30 Career options for those who love Sports

There is an outstanding saying that if you adore what you do, you'll never need to work a single day in your life. Along these lines, you adore sport, and you cherish playing it, watching it, and drawing analysis upon it. What's more, even though you are not planning to turn into an expert competitor or sports individual, you would effectively have a worthwhile vocation around the globe of sport. Worldwide, sport is one of the quickest developing ventures with gross incomes in billions of dollars. Closer home, from being a cricket driven nation, India has now genuinely turned into a medium for various games. There are many associations for Football, Hockey, Kabaddi, volleyball, badminton, tennis, table tennis, formula 1, bicycle leagues, and the sky is the limit from there. Game in India is anticipated to turn into a Billion-dollar industry soon.

Broadly the careers in sports can be divided into seven categories. These categories are explained below.

Category 1 –Sports Management(Sports plus MBA)

1. **Team Management** –In this, you'll have to take care of your entire team from budgets to marketing.
2. **Social Media Manager** – Social media manager, explains that you'll have to manage the social media accounts of these games and their players.
3. **Event Planner** – It requires skills of event management plus a deep interest in the sports
4. **Sports Marketing** – In this, you'll have to take care of sponsorships, intellectual property and merchandising,
5. **Grassroots Development** – In this, your job requires identifying and developing young players from different countries and making them get associated with organizations such as MRF Pace Academy, Olympic Gold quest
6. **Sports Agencies** – In this you'll be handling business and legal dealings of the players

Category 2 –Sports Medicine and Sports Science(Sports + Biology)

7. **Sports Medicine / Sports Physician–** In this, you require an approved degree in medicine and two years full-time (or equivalent) post-qualification in clinical practice
8. **Sports Physiotherapy/Therapist** – In this, the focus is on player rehabilitation and recovery programs. This is usually a masters program after a bachelors in science or physiotherapy
9. **Sports And Exercise Science** – In this field, you'll learn the physiological, biomechanical, and psychological influences on human performance to design the best exercises for each sport
10. **Sports And Exercise Nutrition** – in this, you'll have to design the nutrition chart for the players according to the sport they play.
11. **Sports Psychology** – They help athletes in many ways, including staying motivated, managing competition pressure, and coping with injury and mental health issues.
12. **Kinesiology / Sports Biomechanics/Biomechanist–** For this, you require a master's program in the 'physics of the sport.'

Category 3 – Sports Coaching and Education

13. **Sports Coaching And Physical Education** – This field requires teaching and coaching practical skills as well as academic and scientific skills. In short, it is a career as a coach
14. **Umpire/ Referee** – This requires extensive knowledge of the rules of the sport you want to become a referee of.
15. **Professor** – In this, you can teach others about Sports Management

Category 4 – Sports + Computer Science / Engineering / Math / Statistics

16. **Sports Analytics** – for this you need to have masters in data science or sports analytics or data analytics from a business school
17. **Sports Technology** – In this, you need to have a knowledge of industrial and product design for sports equipment. The courses are broad-based and cover Sports Science, Design, Technology, and Engineering Science.

Category 5 – Sports Law

18. Sports Law is an umbrella term with elements of labor law, media law, contract law, competition law, and tort law; sports law has emerged as a distinctive discipline of legal practice. Sports law can involve litigation, transactional, and regulatory work. Predominantly contract law. But areas such as Intellectual Property, competition law, media law, sport-specific codes and regulations, anti-doping issues, labor law, and taxation also surface frequently. Therefore one can plan to make a career in sports law as well.

Category 6 – Sports Journalism / Public Relations –

19. **Public Relations** – This involves becoming a specialist PR manager for a sports person
20. **Content Creation** – This is a career including Sports writing/blogging with also multimedia content creation coming up
21. **Broadcasting** –
22. **Photojournalism,**
23. **Publishing,**
24. **Sport Show Producer** - You can be a producer of a sports show either on television or any other media
25. **Editor,**
26. **Radio Caster** – become an RJ that specializes in the domain of sport
27. **News Reporter** – A reporter who is a specialist in sport

28. **Social Sciences Research / Market Research** – In this, you can research various domains of sports, e.g., in treatment of eating disorders; improved understanding of the effects of sedentary lifestyles and the benefits of physical activity; academic support to enhance sports coaching; advice to international sports organizations and governments on policies and procedures; guidance and support for elite athletes (both non-disabled and disabled) to achieve their full potential; and the use of exercise in treating health conditions.

Category 7 –

29. **E-sports** – this is now big business. A fortnight and NFL gamers will agree. The esports industry is officially larger than USD 1 billion worldwide
  i. **Athlete/sportsperson** – You can become a cricketer, footballer, or basketball player

Careers in Public administration

A Bachelor's degree in Public Administration can open up a wide range of career opportunities in the public sector. Some of the popular career choices for graduates of BA Public Administration are:

1. **Civil Services:** A degree in Public Administration can serve as a strong foundation for a career in civil services. It can help students develop analytical, communication, and leadership skills which are essential for the role of a civil servant.
2. **Public Policy Analyst:** As a public policy analyst, you will be responsible for analyzing and evaluating government policies and programs to determine their effectiveness. A degree in Public Administration can help you understand the intricacies of the public policy-making process.

3. **Government Relations Specialist:** A government relations specialist is responsible for building and maintaining relationships between government agencies and the public. As a Public Administration graduate, you can help organizations navigate complex government regulations and policies.
4. **Non-profit Management:** Many non-profit organizations require professionals with expertise in public administration to help them manage their operations. As a graduate of BA Public Administration, you can work in areas such as fundraising, public relations, and volunteer management.
5. **Urban Planner:** Urban planners help design and develop cities, towns, and other urban areas. A degree in Public Administration can help you develop the skills and knowledge required to plan and manage urban areas effectively.
6. **Human Resource Manager:** Public Administration graduates can also work as human resource managers in government agencies and non-profit organizations. They can help manage employee relations, benefits, and recruitment.
7. **Public Relations Manager:** Public relations managers are responsible for building and maintaining a positive image of an organization in the public eye. As a Public Administration graduate, you can help government agencies and non-profits manage their public image and reputation.

Overall, a degree in Public Administration can provide you with the necessary skills and knowledge to succeed in a variety of careers in the public sector

Careers in Geology

Geology is the study of the Earth's physical structure, history, and natural resources. A career in geology can lead to a wide range of opportunities, both in the public and private sectors. Some of the careers in geology are:

i. **Geologist:** A geologist is a professional who studies the physical structure, composition, and history of the Earth's crust. They study the processes that shape the Earth, identify natural resources, and advise on issues related to geological hazards.
ii. **Petroleum Geologist:** Petroleum geologists are responsible for the discovery and development of oil and gas reserves. They study the geology of an area to determine the location and size of oil and gas reserves.
iii. **Mining Geologist:** Mining geologists are involved in the exploration, development, and extraction of minerals and other natural resources. They use their knowledge of geology to locate and evaluate mineral deposits.
iv. **Environmental Geologist:** Environmental geologists work to protect the environment by identifying and assessing potential environmental hazards. They study the impact of human activities on the natural environment and help to design plans to mitigate those impacts.
v. **Hydrogeologist:** Hydrogeologists study the movement and storage of groundwater. They help to identify and protect groundwater resources, as well as assess the potential for contamination.
vi. **Geophysicist:** Geophysicists use physics and mathematics to study the physical properties of the Earth, such as gravity, magnetism, and seismic waves. They use this knowledge to map the Earth's subsurface, study earthquakes and other geologic hazards, and explore for natural resources.
vii. **Environmental Consultant:** Environmental consultants use their knowledge of geology to advise clients on environmental issues, such as contaminated sites, land use planning, and waste management.
viii. **Researcher:** Geology researchers work in universities, research institutions, and government agencies to study

various aspects of the Earth, such as climate change, geohazards, and natural resource management.

Overall, a career in geology can offer a diverse range of opportunities and can provide you with the opportunity to make a significant impact on our understanding of the Earth and its resources.

10 Careers in event management

Completing a Bachelor's in Event Management opens up opportunities for a diverse range of careers in the event industry. Here are some of the careers in BA Event Management:

1. **Event Manager:** Event Managers are responsible for planning, organizing and executing events. They need to handle the logistics of the event such as venue booking, vendor coordination, scheduling, and managing event staff. With a degree in event management, you can start your career as an event manager in various event management companies or work as a freelancer.
2. **Event Coordinator:** Event Coordinators work closely with Event Managers to ensure that the event runs smoothly. They help in managing the event, coordinating with the vendors, suppliers, staff and volunteers, ensuring that everything is running as planned. You can work as an event coordinator in event management companies, PR agencies, advertising agencies and hotels.
3. **Wedding Planner:** Wedding planning is a highly specialized area of event management that requires specific skills and knowledge. Wedding planners assist clients with the planning and execution of their wedding. This includes everything from venue selection, vendor management, designing invitations, and decorations, and so on.

4. **Conference Planner:** Conference Planners specialize in organizing conferences, exhibitions, and seminars. They are responsible for coordinating with the vendors, organizing the venue, arranging for catering, and overseeing the entire event.
5. **Public Relations Executive:** Public Relations Executives specialize in promoting a company or individual's image by planning and executing events such as press conferences, product launches, and other promotional events. They work closely with the media to ensure that the event gets the necessary coverage.
6. **Fundraiser:** Fundraisers are responsible for raising funds for various causes by organizing events such as charity auctions, galas, and other events. They work with non-profit organizations to help them achieve their fundraising goals.
7. **Entertainment Manager:** Entertainment Managers are responsible for managing and organizing entertainment events such as concerts, music festivals, and sporting events. They handle everything from booking artists, coordinating with the vendors, and overseeing the event.
8. **Exhibition Designer:** Exhibition Designers specialize in designing the exhibition spaces for trade shows, art exhibitions, and museums. They create a visually appealing space that showcases the products or artworks effectively.
9. **Brand Activations Specialist:** Brand Activations Specialists are responsible for promoting a brand by planning and executing events such as product launches, roadshows, and experiential marketing campaigns. They work closely with the marketing team to ensure that the event aligns with the brand's goals and values.
10. **Social Media Manager:** Social Media Managers are responsible for managing a company or individual's social media accounts. They work with the event management

team to create social media campaigns that promote the event and increase attendance.

6 Careers in Foreign Trade

If you're intrigued by the world of international trade, then a Bachelor of Foreign Trade (BFT) might just be the perfect course for you! This course offers a diverse range of subjects and practical exposure, and it also provides numerous career opportunities in the field of global commerce. So, what kind of careers can you expect to pursue with a BFT degree? Well, let's take a look!

1. One popular career path is that of an **International Trade Analyst**. These professionals analyze global market trends and recommend strategies for businesses to enter foreign markets.
2. Another exciting career option is that of an **International Marketing Manager**, who develops and implements marketing strategies for businesses looking to expand their market internationally. They conduct market research, identify customer needs, and develop advertising campaigns that cater to different cultures.
3. If you're interested in providing guidance and advice to businesses looking to expand their operations internationally, you might consider a career as an **International Business Consultant**. These professionals help businesses navigate the cultural, legal, and regulatory differences between countries, and recommend strategies to overcome these barriers.
4. You might be more interested in a career as an **Export Manager**, overseeing the export of goods and services to foreign markets.
5. **Global Supply Chain Managers** are also in high demand in the world of international business. They manage relationships with suppliers, distributors, and customers, and optimize the supply chain for maximum efficiency and profitability.

6. Finally, if you have a keen eye for detail and a talent for navigating complex regulations, you might consider a career as a **Trade Compliance Manager**. These professionals ensure that businesses comply with international trade regulations and laws, avoiding legal issues and fines.

In conclusion, a Bachelor of Foreign Trade can provide an excellent foundation for students who are passionate about global trade and commerce. Not only does it offer a diverse range of subjects and practical exposure, but it also opens up a world of exciting career opportunities in the field of international business.

10 Careers for Commerce with Maths

The intersection of commerce and mathematics offers a multitude of exciting career paths for those who love numbers and analytics. Here are some of the most in-demand career options in this field:

i. **Actuary:** For those with a passion for risk assessment and financial forecasting, a career as an actuary may be the perfect fit. These professionals use mathematical and statistical methods to evaluate the potential financial consequences of risk and uncertainty, making them invaluable to insurance firms, consulting agencies, and more. To become an actuary, you can pursue a degree in Actuarial Science at a university or register with the Institute of Actuaries in India.

ii. **Chartered Accountant (CA):** Those who enjoy financial management and accounting may want to consider becoming a Chartered Accountant (CA). CAs provide clients with financial advice and oversee their finances, handling tasks such as auditing financial records, preparing tax returns, and ensuring compliance with financial laws and regulations. Aspiring CAs can enroll in the Common Proficiency Test (CPT) provided by the Institute of Chartered Accountants of India (ICAI).

iii. **Financial Analyst:** Financial analysts are experts in using mathematical and statistical tools to evaluate financial data and provide support for investment decisions. They work in a variety of financial institutions, such as banks and investment firms.
iv. **Investment Banker:** For those interested in the exciting world of finance, investment banking may be the perfect career path. Investment bankers use mathematical models and analytical tools to analyze market trends and assist clients in making strategic financial decisions, such as issuing and selling securities to raise capital.
v. **Management Consultant:** Management consultants work with businesses to improve their operations and help them reach their goals. They use mathematical and statistical tools to analyze data and provide recommendations for process improvements.
vi. **Economist:** Economists study the production, distribution, and consumption of goods and services, making predictions about economic trends based on mathematical models and statistical analysis.
vii. **Data Analyst:** In today's data-driven world, the role of a data analyst is more important than ever. Data analysts use mathematical and statistical tools to analyze large sets of data, identifying patterns and trends that can be used to drive business decisions across a range of industries.
viii. **Risk Manager:** Risk managers use mathematical and statistical tools to identify potential risks to a company and develop strategies to mitigate those risks. They work in a variety of industries, such as insurance, banking, and healthcare.
ix. **Financial Planner:** Financial planners use mathematical and statistical tools to help clients manage their finances and plan for the future. They create investment strategies that

align with their clients' financial goals and work to maximize their return on investment.

x. **Statistician:** Statisticians collect, analyze, and interpret data using mathematical and statistical methods. They work in a variety of industries, such as healthcare, government, and research.

10 Career in Science Physics Chemistry Maths Group

Besides the list of all of the careers discussed in for commerce and humanities some career options for students who have studied Science with PCM (Physics, Chemistry, and Mathematics) at the 12th grade level:

1. **Engineering:** Engineering is one of the most popular career options for students with a background in PCM. They can specialize in various fields, such as electrical, mechanical, civil, computer science, aerospace, chemical, and many others.
2. **Architecture:** Architecture is another popular career option for students with PCM. They can study architectural design, planning, and construction, and work on designing buildings and structures.
3. **Information Technology**: Students with PCM can also opt for a career in the field of information technology, where they can work on developing software, designing computer networks, or developing new technologies.
4. **Data Science:** Data science is an emerging field that involves the application of statistics, computer science, and mathematics to analyze large amounts of data. Students with a background in PCM can pursue a career in data science, where they can work on developing algorithms, analyzing data, and creating data visualizations.

5. **Space Technology:** Students with PCM can also pursue a career in space technology, where they can work on designing and developing spacecraft, rockets, and satellites.
6. **Aviation:** Aviation is another career option for students with PCM. They can pursue a career in aircraft design and development, air traffic control, or even become a commercial pilot.
7. **Pure Sciences:** Students with a background in PCM can also opt for a career in pure sciences, such as physics, chemistry, or mathematics. They can work as researchers, professors, or scientists in government or private research organizations.
8. **Defense Services:** Students with PCM can also opt for a career in the defense services, where they can work as engineers, scientists, or technical officers in the army, navy, or air force.
9. **Biotechnology**: Biotechnology is another field where students with PCM can pursue a career. They can work on developing new medicines, improving crop yields, or creating new biotech products.
10. **Renewable Energy:** Students with a background in PCM can also pursue a career in the renewable energy sector, where they can work on developing new technologies and solutions for renewable energy sources, such as solar, wind, or hydro power.

Career in Defence

Are you a student with a strong foundation in Physics, Chemistry, and Mathematics? Did you know that you can also embark on an exciting career in the defense services? Yes, you read that right! By opting for a career in the army, navy, or air force, you can work as an engineer, scientist, or technical officer.

There are two ways to enter the defense services: through the National Defence Academy (NDA) exam or through direct recruitment. If you opt for the former, you'll have to clear a rigorous selection process that includes a written examination, physical fitness test, and an interview. On the other hand, if you go for direct recruitment, you'll be shortlisted based on your educational qualifications and other criteria.

If you're interested in pursuing a technical career in the defense services, you can also explore the Technical Entry Scheme (TES). This program is open to candidates who have completed their 10+2 education with PCM and are between the ages of 16.5 and 19.5 years. The selection process for TES includes a written exam, an interview, and a medical examination.

So, if you have a passion for serving your country and want to utilize your knowledge of physics, chemistry, and mathematics, a career in the defense services could be the perfect fit for you.

17 Career in Science Physics, Chemistry Biology group

Except for courses given in Science PCM group all the above careers are open for students having studies PCB. Here are some career options for students who have studied Science with PCB (Physics, Chemistry, and Biology) at the 12th grade level:

1. **Medicine:** Medicine is one of the most popular career options for students with a background in PCB. They can pursue a career in various fields, such as general practice, surgery, pediatrics, obstetrics and gynecology, cardiology, and many others
2. **Dentistry:** Dentistry is another popular career option for students with PCB. They can specialize in various areas, such as orthodontics, periodontics, endodontics, or oral surgery
3. **Veterinary Science:** Veterinary science is a career option for students who have studied PCB. They can work as

veterinarians, animal nutritionists, animal welfare specialists, or researchers in animal health.

4. **Pharmacy:** Pharmacy is another career option for students with PCB. They can work as pharmacists, pharmacy technicians, or in pharmaceutical research and development.
5. **Biotechnology:** Biotechnology is a rapidly growing field that involves the use of living organisms or biological systems to develop new products and technologies. Students with PCB can work in biotechnology research and development, quality control, and production.
6. **Microbiology:** Microbiology is the study of microorganisms, such as bacteria, viruses, fungi, and parasites. Students with PCB can work in microbiology research, disease control, or pharmaceutical development.
7. **Genetics:** Genetics is the study of genes and heredity. Students with PCB can work in genetic research, genetic counseling, or genetic testing.
8. **Environmental Science:** Environmental science is the study of the natural world and the impact of human activities on the environment. Students with PCB can work in environmental science research, environmental consulting, or environmental policy development.
9. **Forensic Science:** Forensic science is the application of science to legal investigations. Students with PCB can work in forensic science labs, crime scene investigation, or as forensic pathologists.
10. **Nutrition Science:** Nutrition science is the study of food and its effect on the body. Students with PCB can work in nutrition research, public health nutrition, or as registered dietitians.
11. **Nursing:** Nursing is a profession that involves taking care of patients and providing them with medical assistance. Students interested in nursing can become registered nurses,

nurse practitioners, nursing assistants, or licensed practical nurses.

12. **Para Medical:** Para medical professionals are allied healthcare professionals who work under the supervision of medical doctors. Some of the popular para medical careers include medical lab technicians, radiologic technologists, physiotherapists, occupational therapists, and respiratory therapists.
13. **Ayurveda:** Ayurveda is a system of medicine that originated in India and emphasizes natural and holistic approaches to healing. Students interested in Ayurveda can become Ayurvedic doctors, Ayurvedic practitioners, or Ayurvedic therapists.
14. **Unani:** Unani is a system of medicine that originated in Greece and was further developed in India. Unani medicine emphasizes natural remedies and treatments, such as herbal medicines, diet, and exercise. Students interested in Unani medicine can become Unani doctors or Unani practitioners.
15. **Naturopathy:** Naturopathy is a system of medicine that emphasizes natural and non-invasive treatments for various ailments. Naturopathic doctors can use a range of therapies, such as herbal medicines, acupuncture, and massage therapy to treat patients.
16. **Physiotherapy:** Physiotherapy is a healthcare profession that focuses on the prevention, diagnosis, and treatment of movement disorders. Physiotherapists work with patients of all ages who have physical injuries or disabilities, chronic conditions, or neurological disorders. They help patients to improve their movement, manage pain, and regain their strength and mobility. Physiotherapists can work in a variety of settings, such as hospitals, rehabilitation centers, sports clinics, and private practices.
17. **Occupational Therapy:** Occupational therapy is a healthcare profession that focuses on helping people to perform daily

activities and improve their quality of life. Occupational therapists work with patients of all ages who have physical, mental, or emotional disabilities, chronic conditions, or developmental disorders. They help patients to develop the skills and strategies they need to perform daily activities, such as dressing, cooking, and working. Occupational therapists can work in a variety of settings, such as hospitals, rehabilitation centers, schools, and community clinics.

Chapter 6

ENTREPRENEURSHIP AS CAREER

Oh, the world of entrepreneurship! It's one of the most thrilling and constantly evolving fields out there. In our fast-paced and ever-changing world, entrepreneurship offers a path to infinite possibilities and opportunities for innovation, growth, and success. And guess what? India, with its population of over 1.3 billion, has emerged as a hot spot for entrepreneurial activity in recent years. With more and more startups popping up and a supportive ecosystem for entrepreneurship, India is quickly becoming a dream destination for aspiring young entrepreneurs like you.

What makes entrepreneurship such an appealing career option for an undergraduate first-year student, you ask? Well, for starters, it offers the chance to chase your passions and create something truly meaningful and impactful. Plus, it's like a hands-on internship with the least amount of risk, allowing you to test the waters and gain experience with small ventures before diving into something bigger. And the best part? Your peers, professors, friends, and college are all right there to support you, cheer you on, and provide a wealth of resources to make the journey easier.

But wait, there's more! Entrepreneurship offers a pathway to success and fulfillment by giving individuals the power to take control of their lives and build a career around their interests and passions. Not to mention the fact that entrepreneurs have the potential to make a real difference in the world.

Of course, becoming a successful entrepreneur requires certain skills and qualities. Passion for your work, a willingness to take risks, creativity and innovation, adaptability, resilience, and strong communication and leadership skills are just a few of the traits you'll need to succeed. And let's not forget about the ability to handle uncertainty and ambiguity, as the entrepreneurial journey is often full of unpredictable twists and turns.

All in all, the world of entrepreneurship is a dynamic and exhilarating field that offers endless opportunities for growth and achievement. With India leading the charge as a hub of entrepreneurial activity, there's never been a better time for undergraduate students to explore the possibilities and kick-start a career that is both fulfilling and rewarding. With the right skills, qualities, and support system in place, you too can turn your entrepreneurial dreams into a reality and make a positive impact in the world.

Of course, becoming a successful entrepreneur requires certain skills and qualities. Passion for your work, a willingness to take risks, creativity and innovation, adaptability, resilience, and strong communication and leadership skills are just a few of the traits you'll need to succeed. And let's not forget about the ability to handle uncertainty and ambiguity, as the entrepreneurial journey is often full of unpredictable twists and turns.

Entrepreneurship is a journey that requires continuous learning and growth. Higher education plays a critical role in this journey, as it equips aspiring entrepreneurs with the knowledge and skills necessary to succeed in the business world.

Specialized programs in entrepreneurship offered by higher education institutions are one of the ways that aspiring entrepreneurs can gain valuable insights and skills. These programs often include courses on entrepreneurship, innovation, and business management. They may also provide opportunities for students to work with real-world clients, develop business plans, and gain hands-on experience. Additionally, some universities and colleges have entrepreneurship centers that serve as incubators for startups and provide access to funding, mentorship, and other resources.

Higher education also provides access to a network of like-minded individuals, such as professors, alumni, and fellow students. This network can be a valuable resource for building connections, finding mentors, and seeking advice. It is a time when the support of peers and professors can help you grow and thrive.

Entrepreneurship offers several pathways, including starting a business from scratch, buying an existing business or franchise, working for a startup or a small business, and pursuing entrepreneurship as a side gig while working a full-time job. Mini company can also help in this regard as it works within the college premises. Regardless of the pathway chosen, lifelong learning is critical for staying ahead of the curve. It is essential to continuously learn and adapt to new trends and technologies.

Lifelong learning involves acquiring new skills, knowledge, and insights throughout one's career, even after graduation. It is an investment in recreation and learning that helps entrepreneurs balance their personal and professional lives while continuing to grow. As a lifelong learner myself, I have continuously added laurels and experiences through formal and informal education programs. This has helped me grow from one of the crowd to one in the crowd, and I firmly believe that it can do the same for aspiring entrepreneurs.

Starting a Mini Company

Starting a mini company or side hustle is undoubtedly one of the best ways to gain practical experience and test the waters of entrepreneurship. It offers a golden opportunity to apply theoretical knowledge into real-life situations and gain hands-on experience in creating and running a business. A mini company is a small-scale venture that an individual can start with minimal investment and resources, and it can be used to gain valuable experience in a low-risk environment.

When starting a mini company, there are several key steps to follow in order to maximize the learning experience and set yourself up for success. The first step is to define the problem that your product or service will solve. This involves identifying a need in the market that is not currently being met, and developing a solution that addresses that need. This step requires extensive research and analysis to ensure that your solution is viable and marketable.

Once you have identified the problem and developed a solution, the next step is to identify your target audience. This involves understanding the demographic and psychographic characteristics of your potential customers, and tailoring your marketing and sales strategy to appeal to them. This step is critical for ensuring that you are able to effectively reach your intended market and generate sales.

The third step is to develop a Minimum Viable Product (MVP), which is a simplified version of your product or service that can be used to test your assumptions and gather feedback. The MVP is a key component of the Lean Startup methodology, which emphasizes the importance of validating assumptions through experimentation and iteration. Once you have developed your MVP, you will test it with potential customers and gather feedback to inform future development.

Based on the feedback gathered from testing your MVP, you will need to decide whether to persevere or pivot. Persevering means continuing to develop and refine your product or service based on the feedback you have received, while pivoting involves making a significant change to your business model or approach based on the feedback you have received. This step requires careful consideration and analysis, as it will impact the future direction of your business.

After determining your product or service and testing it with your target audience, the next step is to create a business model. This involves outlining how you will generate revenue, what expenses you will incur, and how you will market and sell your product or service. Developing a solid business model is critical for the success of your mini company, as it will ensure that you are able to generate profits and sustain your business over the long-term.

The final steps are to look for customers and sell your product or service. This involves developing a marketing and sales strategy that is tailored to your target audience, and leveraging various channels to reach potential customers. Selling your product or service is the ultimate goal of your mini company, and is a critical step in validating your business model and generating revenue.

In conclusion, starting a mini company is an excellent way to gain practical experience in entrepreneurship. By following the steps outlined above, you can create a valuable learning experience that will provide you with a taste of the life of an entrepreneur and help you understand the challenges and rewards of running your own business.Mini companies are a great example of experiential learning, which is an effective way of learning through practical experiences. It allows individuals to learn, reflect, generalize, and implement. It lets individuals apply their theoretical knowledge in real-life situations and develop critical thinking and problem-solving skills.

Facebook is an excellent example of a mini company that grew to be a giant. It was started in a dorm room, and it is now one of the biggest companies in the world. It shows the potential that mini companies have to grow and become significant businesses.

In addition, starting a mini company or side hustle can be done while pursuing higher education or a full-time job. It can be an excellent way to explore your interests and passions, and create something meaningful and impactful. Furthermore, it can provide additional income and serve as a platform for building a network of contacts and potential customers.

A career in entrepreneurship has several benefits that make it an attractive career option for many individuals. Some of the benefits include being your own boss, having control over your career trajectory, and the potential for financial gain. Additionally, entrepreneurship provides the opportunity to create something meaningful and impactful that can positively affect the lives of others.

There are several ways to launch your entrepreneurial career. One way is to start a mini company or a side hustle, as discussed earlier, which allows you to gain practical experience and test the waters of entrepreneurship. Another way is to find a mentor who can guide and advise you in your entrepreneurial journey. Additionally, attending workshops and events related to entrepreneurship can provide valuable resources and networking opportunities.

Several resources and support are available to aspiring entrepreneurs. Universities and colleges often have entrepreneurship centers, which serve as incubators for startups and provide access to funding, mentorship, and other resources. Additionally, there are various organizations and programs that support entrepreneurship, such as accelerators and pitch competitions. These resources can provide valuable funding, mentorship, and networking opportunities that can aid in launching and growing a successful entrepreneurial career.

In conclusion, a career in entrepreneurship has several benefits and can provide the opportunity to create something meaningful and impactful. Launching an entrepreneurial career can be done through starting a mini company or side hustle, finding a mentor, attending workshops and events related to entrepreneurship, and accessing resources and support from organizations and programs. By utilizing these resources and gaining practical experience, aspiring entrepreneurs can successfully launch and grow their businesses.

Chapter 7

COURSES FOR CAREER OPTIONS

Hello there, fellow future trailblazers! Are you ready to explore how the subjects we study in school can impact our career choices? In the previous chapter, we looked at the wide range of career options available based on our passions and interests. Now, let's focus on mapping these options according to our potential, personality, with courses we need to pursue to achieve our goals.

Sadly, the traditional education system has limited our options by grouping subjects into "streams" and offering only a fixed number of choices within each stream. This narrow approach often leads to a lack of exposure to different subjects and potential careers. But fear not, my friends, as the new national education policy of 2020 is trying to break away from this outdated system.

With the new policy, students will have more flexibility in choosing the subjects they want to study, regardless of their "stream". This means that you can combine your interests in, say, music and mathematics, or biology and business, and chart your own unique academic and career path.

As you approach the end of your school journey, it's essential to understand the wide range of courses available to you after 12th. The right course can have a significant impact on your career and shape your future. So, let's dive in and explore the six groups of courses that you can choose from

A. **Professional Courses:** The first group of courses that you can opt for are the professional courses. These courses require you to enroll in an institute and prepare for exams like CA, CS, Cost, and work, among others. These courses provide a structured approach to learning and can lead to excellent career prospects. If you're someone who's always had a strong inclination towards a specific field, then a professional course could be the right fit for you.
B. **Bachelor's Degree Courses:** The second group of courses that you can explore are Bachelor's degree courses. These courses are available across all streams like B.Tech, B.Sc, B.Com, and BA, to name a few. You can choose to pursue an honors or pass degree, depending on your potential and career aspirations. Bachelor's degree courses offer a broad range of subjects to study and can open up various career opportunities in different fields.
C. **Integrated Courses:** The third group of courses available are integrated courses. These courses provide students with dual courses, saving time and cost while providing an excellent opportunity for early specialization and holistic development. Integrated courses are available across various fields, such as law, engineering, management, journalism, science, humanities, agriculture, fine arts, and design, to name a few. Some popular integrated courses include BA LLB, B.Tech + M.Tech, MBBS + MD, BBA + MBA, and B.Sc + M.Sc.
D. **Hybrid Courses:** The fourth group of courses available are hybrid courses. These courses are gaining popularity among students as they offer a unique combination of subjects, providing students with a diverse range of skills and knowledge. These courses offer a niche area of work, helping you establish yourself early as an expert. Popular hybrid courses include biotechnology and management, computer science and business administration, engineering and management,

psychology and business administration, and fashion designing and management.

E. **Diploma and ITI Courses:** The fifth group of courses available are diploma and ITI courses. These courses provide vocational training and are ideal for those looking to develop practical skills and learn about a specific industry. These courses are often provided by private institutes and ITIs. Diploma course can take anywhere from six months to two years to complete

F. **Certificate Courses:** The sixth group of courses available are certificate courses. These courses are short-term and focus on developing specific skills. They are ideal for those looking to add skills to their existing knowledge or to explore a new field of interest. Certificate courses are often provided by universities and private institutes. Certificate courses are typically shorter in duration than diploma courses. They can range from a few weeks to a few months, depending on the institution and the specific course. Some certificate courses are designed to be completed in as little as four to six weeks, while others may take up to six months.

As you can see, there is an abundance of courses available for students after 12th, and it's important to choose a course that aligns with your interests and career aspirations. Understanding the six groups of courses available will help you make an informed decision and choose the right course for you. So, explore your options and take the first step towards your dream career!

Let's take a dive into the world of opportunities that await you after your 12th standard. As a seasoned career coach, I'm frequently approached by students and their parents for career guidance based on their chosen streams of study. And I can tell you one thing for sure, the choices can be overwhelming! That's why I've simplified it for you by breaking down the options into specific categories.

If you're a Science student with Physics, Chemistry, and Mathematics, don't fret! I've got a whole list of ideal career options just for you. And if you're more inclined towards Biology, there's a whole other realm of possibilities waiting to be explored.

The same applies to students from the Commerce and Humanities streams, as well as those looking for "common careers" that are suitable for students from any stream. With so many options to choose from, the possibilities are endless! So, let's take a closer look at each group and discover what exciting opportunities are available to you.

But remember, these categories are just a starting point. Many careers require a mix of subjects or skills, and there are plenty of options out there that don't fit into a particular stream. A career in journalism, for example, could be open to students from any stream as long as they have excellent writing and communication skills.

At my career coaching service, I'm passionate about helping you navigate the world of career choices. I hope that by breaking down the available options into manageable categories, I can provide a starting point for you to begin your career exploration journey. So, whether you're studying Science, Commerce, or Humanities, there's a world of possibilities out there waiting for you. And that's why I've divided them into six different streams to help you find your dream career. Let's go out there and conquer the world!

1. Common careers for all streams

Are you feeling lost and overwhelmed by the daunting task of choosing a career path that aligns with your passion and potential? Fear not, as there are numerous career options that are open to students from any stream! Let's explore some exciting career paths that you can pursue, regardless of whether you're studying Science, Commerce, or Humanities.

a. **Bachelor of Liberal Studies** is an interdisciplinary undergraduate degree program that offers students a broad-based education by combining courses from different academic disciplines. This degree program is designed to give students a well-rounded education and the flexibility to customize curriculum and explore various areas of study. Students can choose from a wide range of courses in fields like history, literature, philosophy, political science, economics, and social sciences. A Bachelor of Liberal Studies degree can prepare students for a wide range of careers in various fields, including communications, education, public service, social work, and law. Additionally, students who graduate with a Bachelor of Liberal Studies degree often have the skills and knowledge necessary to pursue graduate studies in a variety of fields, including law, social sciences, humanities, and education. Mostly private universities provide this course in India.

b. **Bachelor of Journalism and Mass Communication (BJMC)** is a three-year undergraduate degree program that provides students with the knowledge and skills necessary for a career in the field of media and communication. The course covers a wide range of topics such as media ethics, media laws, public relations, advertising, film studies, radio production, television production, and more. After completing a BJMC course, graduates can pursue a career in various fields like journalism, advertising, public relations, broadcasting, digital media, and more. Some of the popular job roles that BJMC graduates can pursue include:

    i. News Anchor
    ii. Journalist
    iii. Reporter
    iv. Editor

v. Public Relations Specialist
  vi. Advertising Manager
  vii. Radio Jockey
  viii. Video Editor
  ix. Content Writer
  x. Social Media Manager

  A few universities and private institutes provide **diploma courses in journalism and mass media.** These courses are typically shorter in duration than full-fledged degree programs and provide students with the necessary skills and knowledge to kickstart their careers in the field of media and communication. he duration of diploma courses in journalism and mass media varies depending on the university and the program's curriculum. Some diploma courses may be completed in six months, while others may extend up to two years.

c. **Bachelor of Travel and Tourism (BTTM)** is an undergraduate degree program designed for students who want to make a career in the travel and tourism industry. After completing a BTTM course, graduates can pursue a career in various fields related to travel and tourism, such as tour operators, travel agencies, hotels, airlines, tourism boards, and more. Some of the popular job roles that BTTM graduates can pursue include:
   i. Travel consultant
   ii. Tour operator
   iii. Tourism manager
   iv. Hotel manager
   v. Event manager
   vi. Flight attendant
   vii. Travel writer
   viii. Customer service representative
   ix. Tour guide

x. Travel and tourism marketer

Overall, a BTTM course provides students with a comprehensive understanding of the travel and tourism industry and equips them with the necessary skills to succeed in this dynamic and exciting field. The course opens up a plethora of career opportunities for graduates and provides them with a fulfilling and rewarding career in the travel and tourism industry.

In addition to a bachelor's degree in travel and tourism, there are diploma and certificate courses available for students who wish to gain specialized knowledge and skills in the field. These courses are typically of shorter duration and focus on specific areas of the travel and tourism industry, such as tour guiding, hotel management, or airline operations.

d. **Bachelor's degree in Public Relations** is a comprehensive degree program that prepares students for a career in the dynamic and ever-changing field of Public Relations. With excellent communication skills and the ability to build strong relationships, students can pursue a career in PR that can help individuals and organizations communicate effectively with the public, manage their reputation, and maintain a positive image. A Bachelor's degree in Public Relations prepares students for a variety of career opportunities, including PR specialist, media relations specialist, corporate communications specialist, social media manager, and event coordinator.

While a diploma in Public Relations is offered by many institutes such as YMCA and Bhartiya Vidhya Mandir, pursuing a Bachelor's degree in Public Relations is a popular option among students who wish to build a solid foundation in PR principles and practices. However, it is important to note that having a degree is not mandatory to pursue a career in PR. The industry values skills, experience, and networking equally.

e. While it is true that entrepreneurship doesn't necessarily require a degree, obtaining knowledge and skills through formal education can significantly enhance your entrepreneurial journey. **A Bachelor's degree in Entrepreneurship** is an excellent way to gain comprehensive knowledge and hands-on experience in this field.

For those interested in entrepreneurship and business, a **Bachelor's degree in Business Administration (BBA)** can serve as a gateway to a successful career in management, finance, marketing, or human resources. The program is designed to help students develop their entrepreneurial mindset and acquire the necessary skills to start and manage a business venture. Admission to a Bachelor's degree in Entrepreneurship program is generally based on an entrance exam conducted by state and private universities. Some institutions may also consider factors such as academic performance, extracurricular activities, and work experience.

With a Bachelor's degree in Entrepreneurship, graduates can pursue careers as entrepreneurs, start-ups, or work in managerial positions in established organizations. They can also choose to pursue advanced degrees such as a Master's in Business Administration (MBA) or other related fields. A degree in entrepreneurship provides students with a solid foundation to pursue their business goals and achieve their dreams of running a successful venture.

f. **Bachelor's degree in Law** is a great choice for students who are passionate about the legal field and want to pursue a career as a lawyer, legal advisor, or judge. 5-year integrated courses such as BA LLB and BBALLB are available for students who wish to enter this profession. Admission to these courses is usually granted based on the Common Law Admission Test (CLAT), which is conducted at the national level.

Upon graduation, students with a degree in Law can pursue a variety of career paths, including litigation, corporate law, public interest law, and legal academia. Some graduates also choose to pursue further education in law and earn a Master's or Doctoral degree.

g. **Bachelor's degree in Architecture or Interior Designing** can be an excellent option for creative individuals who want to design beautiful and functional spaces. These courses typically take four to five years to complete, and admission is based on an entrance exam conducted by the respective universities. Few universities and private institutes offer diploma in interior designing.

Upon graduation, students with a degree in Architecture or Interior Designing can pursue a variety of career paths, including working at architecture and design firms, real estate development companies, and construction companies. They can also choose to start their own businesses or pursue further education in related fields such as urban planning, environmental design, or historic preservation.

h. **Bachelor's degree in Design** is an excellent option for students who are interested in creating functional and aesthetically pleasing products, environments, or experiences. There are many different types of design programs available, such as graphic design, industrial design, fashion design, and interior design.

Upon graduation, students with a degree in Design can pursue a variety of career paths, such as working for design firms, advertising agencies, marketing departments, or starting their own businesses. Graduates may also choose to work in fields related to design, such as product development, web design, or user experience design.

i. **Bachelor's degree in Fashion Design** typically focuses on training students in the creation of clothing and accessories, including designing and pattern-making, while incorporating knowledge of textiles and technology. **Textile Design degrees** focus more specifically on the study of fabrics, including printing, weaving, and dyeing. **Leather Design** programs center on creating products such as shoes, bags, and jackets using leather, while **Accessory Design** courses focus on designing jewellery, belts, hats, and other accessories. **Jewellery Design** programs focus solely on designing and creating unique pieces of jewellery. **Knitwear Design** degrees specialize in creating clothing items made from knit fabrics. Meanwhile, a **degree in Fashion Communication** focuses on building skills in fashion journalism, public relations, and advertising, as well as the use of technology and social media to promote fashion brands. A **degree in Apparel Production** teaches students how to manage the manufacturing and production of fashion products. **Fashion Management** programs provide a broad understanding of the fashion industry, including marketing, merchandising, and retailing. Finally, a **degree in Fashion Technology** covers the use of technology in fashion design and production, including computer-aided design, virtual reality, and digital printing.

Numerous institutes offer these programs, including prestigious institutions like the National Institute of Design (NID), National Institute of Fashion Technology (NIFT), Indian Institute of Fashion Technology (IIFT), as well as private and government universities. These institutes offer both Bachelor's and Diploma courses.

j. If you are interested in languages, you could pursue a **Bachelor's degree in Foreign Language.** This program can provide a deep understanding of a particular language, including its grammar, syntax, and culture, and can lead to careers in translation, interpretation, or international relations. Many central, state, and private universities offer these programs, along with diploma courses.

k. **Bachelor of Social Work (BSW)** degree is the most common educational pathway to become a social worker. This degree program prepares students with the knowledge, skills, and values needed to work effectively in the social work field. Upon completing a BSW degree, you can pursue a variety of social work careers, such as becoming a child welfare worker, a school social worker, a community outreach worker, a mental health counselor, or a non-profit program manager, to name a few. Depending on your interests and goals, you may choose to specialize in a specific area of social work, such as healthcare, substance abuse, or family services.

Bachelor's degree programs in social work are offered by many universities and colleges, both public and private. Some of the well-known institutes in India that offer BSW courses include Tata Institute of Social Sciences, Delhi University, Madras School of Social Work, and Christ University. The duration of these programs is typically 3-4 years, depending on the institute and curriculum.

l. **Bachelor of Arts (B.A.) and Bachelor of Education (B.Ed.)** is 5 year integrated program that combines the study of a subject in the arts stream, such as English, history, or economics, with the necessary pedagogical training required to become a teacher. This program provides a deeper understanding of a particular subject and prepares students to effectively teach the same to school students.

Apart from the B.A. B.Ed., some universities in India also offer integrated **B.Sc. B.Ed.** programs for those interested in teaching science subjects. These programs provide in-depth knowledge of science subjects, along with the required pedagogical training to become a teacher.

In India, the State Council of Educational Research and Training (SCERT) has District Institutes of Education and Training (DIET) to prepare teachers for elementary education. These institutes offer a **Diploma in Elementary Education (D.El.Ed.)** program, which provides training to become a primary school teacher. The D.El.Ed. program is a 2-year course that covers topics such as child development, pedagogy, and teaching methodology.

In recent years, with the introduction of the National Education Policy, there has been an increase in the availability of 5-year integrated B.A. B.Ed. and B.Sc. B.Ed. programs in India. These programs aim to create well-rounded teachers with a deep understanding of both the subject they teach and the pedagogical skills required to be an effective teacher

m. **Bachelor of Library Science (BLib)** is an undergraduate program that provides students with a comprehensive understanding of library science, library management, and information science. This program is designed for individuals who are interested in pursuing a career in the library sector and wish to develop the necessary knowledge and skills required to succeed in this field.

After completing the BLib program, graduates can pursue careers as librarians, information scientists, and knowledge managers. They can work in a range of settings, including universities, research institutions, government agencies, and private corporations. In addition to traditional library roles, graduates can also pursue careers in related fields, such as archives, records management, and information architecture.

n. **Bachelor in Yoga** is a program that focuses on the ancient practice of yoga, which combines physical postures, breathing exercises, and meditation to promote physical and mental well-being. This program is ideal for students who are passionate about yoga and want to explore opportunities to become yoga instructors, yoga therapists, or even own a yoga studio. They can work in a range of settings, including yoga studios, health and wellness centers, and fitness clubs. Graduates can also pursue advanced studies in yoga, such as a Master's in Yoga or a specialized training in a specific form of yoga, such as Hatha yoga, Ashtanga yoga, or Iyengar yoga

o. **Bachelor of Vocation (B.Voc)** is an undergraduate degree program that is designed to provide students with job-oriented training and skill development in specific fields. The program is typically offered by universities, colleges, and institutes in collaboration with industry partners to ensure that students acquire the skills and knowledge required to excel in their chosen profession.

The duration of the B.Voc program is typically three years, but some institutes may offer a four-year program with a specialization in a particular vocational field. The program is designed to equip students with job-ready skills that are required by the industry, making them highly employable. Upon completion of the B.Voc program, graduates can pursue careers in a range of industries, depending on the vocational field they have chosen. They can work as technicians, supervisors, managers, trainers, or entrepreneurs. The program prepares graduates to be self-sufficient and to start their own businesses, which is an added advantage for those who wish to become entrepreneurs.

p. **Bachelor in Hotel Management (BHM)** is an undergraduate degree program that focuses on preparing students for a career in the hospitality industry. The program is typically offered by universities, colleges, and institutes and provides students with a broad understanding of various aspects of the hospitality industry. The duration of the BHM program is typically four years, and some institutes may offer a three-year program with a specialization in a particular area of the hospitality industry. Graduates of the BHM program can pursue careers in various areas of the hospitality industry. They can work as hotel managers, food and beverage managers, event planners, tour operators, or chefs. They can also work in other sectors such as airline catering, cruise ship hospitality, and healthcare catering. Hotel management is also offered in diploma and certificate courses in parts like diploma in chef, front office etc.

q. **Bachelor of Fine Arts (BFA)** is an undergraduate degree program that focuses on developing students' artistic skills and creativity. It is a popular degree program for students who are interested in pursuing a career in the visual or performing arts. Upon completing a BFA program, students will be prepared for a wide range of careers in the arts. Some may pursue careers as professional artists, while others may work in fields such as art education, art therapy, arts administration, graphic design, advertising, or film and television production. The skills and knowledge gained in a BFA program can be applied in a variety of fields, making it a versatile and valuable degree for creative individuals.

r. **Bachelor of Performing Arts (BPA)** is an undergraduate degree program that focuses on developing students' skills in the performing arts. It is a popular degree program for students who are interested in pursuing a career in theatre, dance, music, or other related fields. Upon completing a BPA program, students will be prepared for a wide range of careers in the performing arts. Some may pursue careers as professional performers in theatre, dance, or music. Others may work in fields such as arts administration, event management, or arts education

s. **Bachelor's degree in Photography** is an undergraduate program that aims to provide students with a comprehensive understanding of the art and science of photography. Through this program, students are equipped with the necessary technical and artistic skills to create and capture stunning visuals. Some of the top institutes that offer Bachelor's degree in Photography in India include The Indian Institute of Digital Art and Animation, Kolkata; Osmania University, Hyderabad; Delhi College of Photography, Delhi; Jawaharlal Nehru Architecture and Fine Arts University, Hyderabad; and National Institute of Photography, Mumbai. These institutes provide students with both theoretical knowledge and practical experience through various workshops, field trips, and internships. Graduates of this program can explore various career opportunities such as commercial photographer, photojournalist, art director, photo editor, and more. Many institutes, particularly ITI and private institutions, offer this course as both diploma and certificate courses.

t. **Bachelor's degrees in Animation and VFX Design**, Graphics and Digital Media, Visual Media, Multimedia and Animation, and Media Studies (Hons) are undergraduate programs that provide students with a comprehensive understanding of different aspects of the media industry. These programs typically cover a wide range of topics including 2D and 3D animation, visual effects, graphic design, digital media production, web design, media writing, and more. A Bachelor's degree in Animation and VFX Design is ideal for individuals interested in a career in the animation and visual effects industry. This program is designed to teach students the principles of animation, including character animation, special effects, and storyboarding. The program is offered by various private institutes in India. Many institutes, particularly ITI and private institutions, offer this course as both diploma and certificate courses.

u. **Bachelor's degree in Graphics and Digital Media** is designed to prepare students for careers in the graphic design and digital media industries. The program provides students with a comprehensive understanding of graphic design software, typography, digital imaging, and digital media production. Institutes in India that offer this program include: National Institute of Design (NID), and other private institutes and universities. Many institutes, particularly ITI and private institutions, offer this course as both diploma and certificate courses.

v. **Bachelor's degree in Visual Media** is designed for individuals interested in pursuing a career in film, television, or advertising. This program covers topics like cinematography, film production, television production, and advertising. Private Institutes in India. Many institutes, particularly ITI and private institutions, offer this course as both diploma and certificate courses.

w. **Bachelor's degree in Multimedia and Animation** is designed to provide students with a broad understanding of the multimedia industry. This program covers topics like animation, graphic design, web design, and multimedia production. Institutes in India that offer this program include:Manipal Academy of Higher Education (MAHE), Manipal and other private universities . Many institutes, particularly ITI and private institutions, offer this course as both diploma and certificate courses.

x. **Bachelor's degree in Media Studies (Hons)** is designed for individuals interested in pursuing a career in media and journalism. The program covers topics like media writing, media ethics, media law, and media management. Institutes in India that offer this program include:Delhi University, Jamia Millia Islamia, Delhi and others Many institutes, particularly

ITI and private institutions, offer this course as both diploma and certificate courses.

List of common courses offered in Diploma

These courses are offered as diplomas or certificate courses in various institutes, mostly ITI or private.

1. **Video production and cinematography** courses are designed to teach the technical aspects of creating videos. These courses provide a comprehensive understanding of camera operation, lighting, sound, and editing. Students will learn to use video production equipment, frame a shot, use lighting and sound, and edit and present a video project. The courses cover different types of videos, such as documentaries, short films, music videos, and more. These courses prepare students for careers in fields like film production, advertising, corporate video production, and more.
2. **Acting courses** aim to teach the art of acting, including acting techniques, character development, improvisation, voice and movement, and more. The courses provide an opportunity for students to develop their performance skills and work on a variety of scenes and projects. Students will also learn about the business of acting, including how to audition, how to market themselves, and how to work with agents and casting directors. Acting courses can prepare students for careers in film, television, theater, and more.
3. To become a **voiceover artist**, individuals need to have a keen sense of tone, pitch, and timing. Voiceover artists provide voiceovers for various media, including commercials, audiobooks, cartoons, and video games. They bring characters to life and captivate the audience.

4. **Food styling** is responsible for making food visually appealing for photographs or videos, such as for cookbooks, advertising campaigns, or social media. Food stylists have an eye for detail and creativity to make food look delicious and tempting.
5. **Cryptography** involves designing and decoding codes and ciphers for secure communication and data protection. Cryptographers must have exceptional analytical skills and be able to think critically to ensure that the codes are secure.
6. **Diploma in Film/TV Set Design** can be pursued to learn the skills required for designing and constructing sets for movies, television shows, and theatrical productions.
7. **Certificate in Costume Design** can provide training in designing and creating costumes for different media.
8. **Diploma in Medical Illustration** can provide training in medical terminology, anatomy, and illustration techniques to create visuals for medical publications.
9. **Certificate in Digital Marketing** can provide training in social media marketing, content marketing, and search engine optimization to promote products or services online.
10. **Certificate in Ethical Hacking** can provide training in computer systems, programming languages, and cybersecurity to identify and fix vulnerabilities in a company's computer systems.
11. **Certificate in Drone Operation** can provide training in technical skills and aviation regulations required for operating unmanned aerial vehicles.
12. **Diploma in Music Therapy** can provide training in music theory and therapy techniques to become a healthcare professional who uses music to help patients improve their physical and mental well-being. Institutes like the National Institute of Open Schooling, and many more offer these courses in India.

13. **Diploma/Certificate in UX Design** trains students in designing user experiences for digital products and services. Institutes like the Indian School of Design and Innovation, Mumbai and the National Institute of Design, Ahmedabad offer these courses.
14. **Diploma/Certificate in Environmental Engineering** provides students with an understanding of environmental problems and solutions, as well as knowledge of regulations and sustainability. Institutes like the Centre for Environmental Planning and Technology University, Ahmedabad and the Indian Institute of Technology, Delhi offer these courses.
15. **Diploma/Certificate in Adventure Guiding** trains students in leading outdoor adventure activities safely and effectively. Institutes like the Himalayan Mountaineering Institute, Darjeeling and the Nehru Institute of Mountaineering, Uttarakhand offer these courses.
16. **Diploma/Certificate in Sommelier Studies**: provides students with knowledge of different types of wines, their characteristics, and how to pair them with food. Institutes like the Institute of Wine and Beverage Studies, Mumbai and the Wine Academy of India, Bangalore offer these courses.
17. **Diploma/Certificate in Pet Grooming:** trains students in grooming pets, including bathing, styling, and health checks. Institutes like the Madras Canine Club, Chennai and the PetGroom Academy, Mumbai offer these courses.

2. Careers after studying humanities in 12th

Besides all the above mentioned careers student who has studies humanities in class 12 can do

a. Bachelor of Arts (BA) -
A Bachelor of Arts (BA) can offer a wide range of subjects to choose from, including but not limited to:

- Anthropology
- Applied Psychology
- Archaeology
- Culinary Arts
- Development Studies
- Development Policy, Planning, and Practice
- Economics
- Education
- English
- Geography
- Global Peace, Security, and Strategic Studies
- Health Administration
- History
- International Relations
- Mass Communication
- Labour Studies
- Liberal Arts
- Linguistics
- Media Studies
- Peace and Conflict Studies
- Political Sciences
- Psychology
- Public Administration
- Public Health
- Sociology
- Theatre Arts
- Travel and Tourism
- Visual Arts
- Women's Studies
- Gender, Culture, and Development Studies

These subjects can provide a comprehensive understanding of various fields and prepare students for careers in diverse industries, including but not limited to education, media, politics, healthcare, tourism, and arts. Different universities and colleges may offer different subjects under the BA program, so it's essential to research and find the one that aligns with your interests and career goals.. Students can choose to specialize in any of these subjects as per their interest. This course is available in almost all the universities be it central, state or private

b. BA language :In India, there are a number of universities and colleges that offer Bachelor of Arts (BA) degree programs in various language and literature subjects. Some of the popular BA language and literature courses available in India are:

BA English Literature

BA Hindi Literature

BA Sanskrit Literature

BA Pali Language

BA Bengali Literature

BA Urdu Literature

BA Punjabi Literature

BA Gujarati Literature

BA Marathi Literature

BA Tamil Literature

BA Telugu Literature

BA Kannada Literature

BA Malayalam Literature

BA Arabic Language and Literature

BA Persian Language and Literature

BA French Language and Literature

BA German Language and Literature

BA Spanish Language and Literature

BA Italian Language and Literature

BA Chinese Language and Literature

BA Japanese Language and Literature

These courses typically cover a range of subjects such as literature, language, linguistics, culture, history, and other related areas. The duration of the course is usually three years, and admission to the program is usually based on merit or through an entrance exam conducted by the respective university or college. Many Universities provide these courses. Scope of careers in Language is discussed in previous chapter

3. Courses for Career in commerce without maths

If you are a student with an interest in the field of commerce, but without a strong mathematical background, you'll be pleased to know that there are plenty of options available to you! And all the above discussed options are also open for you. Let's take a closer look at some of the courses that can help you achieve your career goals.

1. First up is the **Company Secretary (CS)** course, which is offered by the Institute of Company Secretaries of India (ICSI). This course focuses on legal and regulatory compliance, and is ideal for those who are interested in corporate governance.
2. Another popular option is the **Bachelor of Commerce (B.Com)** degree, which is a three-year undergraduate program. This degree offers a wide range of specializations,

such as Accounting and Finance, Banking and Insurance, Business Process Services, Taxation, International Business, and Human Resource Management.
3. For those interested in management and business, the **Bachelor of Business Administration (BBA)** degree is a great choice. This program covers topics such as marketing, finance, human resources, and operations management.
4. The **Bachelor of Management Studies (BMS)** degree is another great option for those interested in management principles and practices, and covers topics such as organizational behavior, marketing, finance, and operations.
5. If you are interested in the application of computer technology in commerce, you may want to consider the **Bachelor of Commerce in Computer Applications (B.Com CA)** degree, which covers topics such as programming, database management, and software development.
6. Other specialized degrees include the **Bachelor of Commerce in E-Commerce (B.Com E-Commerce)**, which focuses on electronic commerce and covers topics such as website development, e-marketing, and e-business,
7. **Bachelor of Commerce in Entrepreneurship (B.Com Entrepreneurship)**, covers the principles of starting and managing a business.
8. For those interested in event planning and management, the **Bachelor of Commerce in Event Management (B.Com Event Management)** is an excellent option. This degree covers topics such as event planning, budgeting, and execution.
9. **Bachelor of Commerce in Hospitality and Tourism Management (B.Com HTM)** degree focuses on hospitality and tourism management, and covers topics such as hotel management, travel and tourism management, and event planning.

10. **Bachelor of Foreign Trade (BFT)** is an exciting and rapidly growing field that focuses on global trade and commerce. If you have an interest in international business and trade, BFT could be an ideal course for you. BFT is a three-year undergraduate program that offers students an in-depth understanding of international trade and business practices. As you can see, there are plenty of courses available to help you achieve your career goals in the field of commerce, even if you do not have a strong mathematical background. So go ahead and explore your options, and choose the course that best suits your interests and career aspirations.

4. Courses for Career in commerce with maths

Students with a background in Commerce with Mathematics in 12th grade have a wide range of courses to choose from. Here are some of the popular courses that they can consider:

18. **Bachelor of Commerce (B.Com)honors** : This is a 3-year undergraduate degree course that covers subjects like accounting, finance, economics, taxation, and business law.
19. **Bachelor of Economics (B.Eco):** This is a 3-year undergraduate degree course that covers topics related to economics, including microeconomics, macroeconomics, econometrics, and statistical analysis.
20. **Bachelor of Business Studies (BBS):** This is a 3-year undergraduate degree course that covers topics related to business, management, and entrepreneurship.
21. **Bachelor of Finance and Accounting (BFA):** This is a 3-year undergraduate degree course that covers accounting, finance, auditing, and taxation.
22. **Chartered Accountancy (CA):** This is a professional course that takes 4-5 years to complete and leads to a career as a

Chartered Accountant. The course covers accounting, taxation, auditing, and financial management.

23. **Company Secretary (CS):** This is a professional course that takes 3-4 years to complete and leads to a career as a Company Secretary. The course covers various aspects of corporate law, governance, and management.
24. **Cost and Management Accountancy (CMA):** This is a professional course that takes 3-4 years to complete and leads to a career as a Cost and Management Accountant. The course covers various aspects of cost accounting, financial management, and management accounting.
25. **Actuarial Science:** This is a professional course that takes 3-4 years to complete and leads to a career as an Actuary. The course covers topics related to risk assessment, probability, statistics, and financial mathematics.
26. **Bachelor of Statistics (B.Stat):** This is a 3-year undergraduate degree course that covers topics related to statistics, probability, data analysis, and mathematical modelling.
27. **Bachelor of Computer Applications (BCA):** This is a 3-year undergraduate degree course that focuses on computer applications and covers subjects like programming, database management, and software development.
28. **Bachelor of Mathematics (B.Math):** This is a 3-year undergraduate degree course that covers various branches of mathematics, including algebra, calculus, geometry, and number theory.
29. **Bachelor of Science in Applied Mathematics (B.Sc. Applied Mathematics):** This is a 3-year undergraduate degree course that covers a wide range of topics related to mathematics, including analysis, topology, logic, and mathematical physics.

These are just a few examples of the many courses that students with Commerce and Mathematics background can pursue. It's important to research and explore different options to find the best fit for your interests and career goals

In the previous chapter, we explored some careers that didn't have a clear-cut course of study. But don't worry, we've got your back!

For all the budding **financial analysts** out there, here's a handy list of courses you can take to pave your way to success:

1. Bachelor's Degree in Finance or Accounting: This is your first step towards becoming a financial analyst. This course covers essential topics like financial statements analysis, financial markets, portfolio management, and financial risk management.
2. Master's in Business Administration (MBA) in Finance: Take your financial analysis game to the next level with an MBA in Finance. This program provides in-depth knowledge and skills required for financial analysis. And as a bonus, it also offers networking and internship opportunities that can boost your job prospects.
3. Chartered Financial Analyst (CFA) Program: If you want to be recognized as a true financial analysis expert, then the CFA program is for you. This professional certification equips you with knowledge in investment analysis, portfolio management, and ethical standards. The program consists of three levels, and you need to pass each level to become a CFA charter holder.
4. Financial Risk Manager (FRM) Program: Risk management is a crucial aspect of financial analysis. This professional certification program offered by the Global Association of Risk Professionals (GARP) equips you with knowledge in financial risk management, credit risk analysis, and operational risk management.

5. Certificate in Investment Banking: Pursuing a certificate in Investment Banking can provide you with knowledge in financial modeling, valuation, and mergers and acquisitions. You can pursue this certificate online or through short-term courses. This certificate will give you an edge over other financial analysts and help you stand out in a crowded job market.

So, there you have it! With these courses under your belt, you'll be well on your way to becoming a financial analysis superstar.

Are you ready to take the world of finance by storm? If your heart is set on becoming **an investment banker**, then here are some courses and programs that you might want to consider:

1. Bachelor's Degree in Finance or Business: To get started in investment banking, a bachelor's degree in finance or business is the way to go. These programs cover essential topics like accounting, corporate finance, economics, and financial markets, which form the foundation of investment banking.
2. Master's in Business Administration (MBA): Take your investment banking skills to the next level with an MBA in finance. These programs offer in-depth knowledge and skills required for investment banking. Plus, you'll get to network with other professionals and participate in internships, which can boost your chances of landing your dream job.
3. Chartered Financial Analyst (CFA) Program: The CFA program is a professional certification that will equip you with the knowledge and skills required for investment analysis, portfolio management, and ethical standards. The program enhances your analytical and quantitative skills, which are essential for investment banking.
4. Investment Banking Certification: There are various investment banking certifications available, such as Certified

Investment Banking Associate (CIBA) or Certified Investment Banking Professional (CIBP). These certifications provide you with specialized knowledge in financial modeling, valuation, and mergers and acquisitions, which are specific to investment banking.
5. Internship Programs: Internship programs offered by investment banks provide practical experience in investment banking. These programs also offer networking opportunities and can enhance your job prospects.

In addition to these courses, it's also essential to develop strong communication and interpersonal skills and gain a solid understanding of global financial markets. With hard work and determination, you'll be on your way to becoming a top-notch investment banker in no time!

5. Courses in Science Physics Chemistry Maths Group

Students with a strong foundation in Physics, Chemistry, and Mathematics (PCM) have a wide range of courses to choose from after completing their 12th grade. They can choose any of the courses above . Besides that here's a list of some of the popular courses that PCM students can opt for:

i. **Engineering**: This is a four-year undergraduate program that covers various specializations such as Computer Science, Electronics and Communication, Mechanical, Civil, and Chemical Engineering.
ii. **Architecture:** This is a five-year undergraduate program that teaches students about designing and planning buildings and other physical structures.
iii. **Bachelor of Science (B.Sc.)**: This is a three-year undergraduate program that covers various specializations such as Physics, Chemistry, Mathematics, Statistics, and Computer Science.

iv. **Bachelor of Information Technology (BIT):** This is a three-year undergraduate program that covers various aspects of information technology such as computer networks, database management, and software development.

v. **Commercial Pilot Training:** This is a three-year training program that provides students with the skills and knowledge required to become a commercial pilot.

vi. **National Defense Academy (NDA)** Training: This is a three-year training program for students who aspire to join the Indian Army, Navy, or Air Force.

vii. **Bachelor of Science in Aviation:** This is a three-year undergraduate program that covers various aspects of aviation such as air traffic control, airport management, and aircraft maintenance.

viii. **BSc Food Technology:** This is a three-year undergraduate program that focuses on the study of food processing, preservation, and safety. Students learn about the various aspects of food science, including food chemistry, microbiology, and nutrition. The program also covers subjects such as food packaging, food engineering, and food quality management. Graduates of this program can work in the food industry, research and development, and food regulatory bodies.

ix. **BSc Geology:** This is a three-year undergraduate program that focuses on the study of the Earth's structure, materials, and processes. Students learn about geology, mineralogy, petrology, paleontology, and geomorphology. The program also covers subjects such as environmental geology, geological engineering, and exploration geophysics. Graduates of this program can work in fields such as mining, oil and gas exploration, environmental consulting, and geotechnical engineering.

x. **BSc Operations Research:** This is a three-year undergraduate program that focuses on the application of mathematical and statistical techniques to optimize business operations and decision-making. Students learn about linear and nonlinear programming, queueing theory, decision analysis, and simulation. The program also covers subjects such as supply chain management, project management, and data analytics. Graduates of this program can work in fields such as logistics, manufacturing, transportation, and finance.

xi. **BSc Metrology:** This is a three-year undergraduate program that focuses on the science of measurement and calibration. Students learn about metrology, dimensional analysis, uncertainty analysis, and calibration procedures. The program also covers subjects such as quality management, measurement systems analysis, and laboratory accreditation. Graduates of this program can work in fields such as manufacturing, aerospace, automotive, and calibration laboratories.

xii. **BSc Anthropology:** This is a three-year undergraduate program that focuses on the study of human cultures, societies, and biological diversity. Students learn about social anthropology, physical anthropology, and cultural anthropology. The program also covers subjects such as archaeology, linguistics, and forensic anthropology. Graduates of this program can work

xiii. **BSc in Data Science** is an undergraduate degree program that aims to provide students with a strong foundation in computer science, statistics, and data analysis. The program focuses on teaching students how to collect, analyze and interpret large sets of data using various techniques and tools. This program typically covers topics such as data mining, machine learning, statistical methods, programming languages, data visualization, and data management. Graduates of this program can pursue a career in fields such as data analysis, data science, business intelligence, and big data.

xiv. **BSc in Business Analytics** is an undergraduate degree program that focuses on developing skills and knowledge in the field of business analytics. This program aims to teach students how to analyze and interpret business data to make informed decisions. The program typically covers topics such as statistics, data visualization, machine learning, database management, and programming languages. Graduates of this program can pursue a career in fields such as business intelligence, data analytics, and management consulting.

xv. **BSc Marine Engineering:** is a four-year undergraduate course that trains students in the design, construction, and maintenance of ships and other ocean-related structures. The course covers topics such as marine propulsion, fluid mechanics, naval architecture, thermodynamics, and marine engineering systems. The aim of the course is to equip students with the technical and practical skills required to work in the marine industry. After completing the course, students can work in various sectors such as shipbuilding, offshore oil and gas, and marine research and development.

xvi. **BSc Nautical Science:** is also a four-year undergraduate course that prepares students for a career in the shipping industry. The course covers topics such as navigation, seamanship, ship stability, cargo handling, and maritime law. The aim of the course is to provide students with the skills and knowledge required to work as deck officers on board ships. After completing the course, students can work in various sectors such as commercial shipping, cruise liners, and naval organizations.

xvii. **BSc Petroleum Technology:** This is a three-year undergraduate course that focuses on the exploration, production, and processing of petroleum products. The course covers topics such as drilling engineering, reservoir engineering, petrochemical processing, and petroleum economics. The aim of the course is to equip students with the technical and practical skills required to work in the oil and gas industry. After completing the course, students can work in various sectors such as oil and gas exploration, production, and

These are just some of the many courses that students with PCM can opt for after completing their 12th grade. It's important to research and explore the various options before making a decision to pursue a course that aligns with their interests and goals.

6. Courses for Career in Science Physics, Chemistry Biology group

Students who have completed their 12th with PCB (Physics, Chemistry, Biology) have a wide range of courses above to choose from. Here are some of the popular courses for students from the PCB group:

1. **MBBS (Bachelor of Medicine and Bachelor of Surgery):** It is a 5.5 years course that includes classroom learning, practical training, and an internship. It is the most popular course for PCB students who aspire to become doctors.
2. **BDS (Bachelor of Dental Surgery):** It is a 4-year undergraduate degree that includes classroom learning, practical training, and an internship. Students who want to become dentists can pursue this course.
3. **B.Pharm (Bachelor of Pharmacy):** It is a 4-year undergraduate course that provides students with knowledge and skills in pharmaceutical science. It covers topics such as drug formulation, drug delivery systems, pharmacology, and pharmacognosy.
4. **B.Sc. Nursing:** It is a 4-year undergraduate course that provides students with knowledge and skills in nursing. It includes classroom learning, practical training, and an

internship. Students who want to pursue a career in nursing can opt for this course.

5. **BAMS (Bachelor of Ayurvedic Medicine and Surgery):** It is a 5.5 years course that includes the study of Ayurveda, the ancient Indian system of medicine. It covers topics such as anatomy, physiology, pharmacology, and pathology.
6. **BHMS (Bachelor of Homeopathic Medicine and Surgery):** It is a 5.5 years course that includes the study of homeopathy, an alternative system of medicine. It covers topics such as homeopathic philosophy, materia medica, and repertory.
7. **B.Sc. Biotechnology:** It is a 3-year undergraduate course that provides students with knowledge and skills in biotechnology. It covers topics such as cell biology, genetics, microbiology, biochemistry, and biostatistics.
8. **B.Sc. Microbiology:** It is a 3-year undergraduate course that provides students with knowledge and skills in microbiology. It covers topics such as bacteriology, virology, mycology, immunology, and molecular biology.
9. **B.Sc. Biochemistry:** It is a 3-year undergraduate course that provides students with knowledge and skills in biochemistry. It covers topics such as enzymology, metabolism, protein structure, and molecular genetics.
10. **B.Sc. Environmental Science:** It is a 3-year undergraduate course that provides students with knowledge and skills in environmental science. It covers topics such as environmental pollution, natural resource management, and climate change.
11. **BSc in Pathology** is an undergraduate degree program that focuses on the study of the nature, causes, and effects of diseases. This program aims to teach students how to diagnose and treat diseases and disorders through laboratory analysis of bodily fluids and tissues. The program typically covers topics such as pathology, microbiology, hematology,

immunology, and biochemistry. Graduates of this program can pursue a career in fields such as medical laboratory technology, diagnostic pathology, and medical research.

12. **BSc in Forensic Science** is an undergraduate degree program that focuses on the application of science to the investigation of crime. The program aims to teach students how to collect and analyze evidence from crime scenes and provide scientific support for criminal investigations. The program typically covers topics such as forensic toxicology, forensic biology, forensic chemistry, crime scene investigation, and criminal law. Graduates of this program can pursue a career in fields such as forensic science, crime scene investigation, and forensic toxicology.

13. **B.Sc. Nursing**: B.Sc. Nursing is an undergraduate course that typically lasts for four years. This course is designed to provide students with the knowledge and skills necessary to become a registered nurse.

14. **Bachelor of Physiotherapy:** This is an undergraduate course that typically lasts for four and a half years. This course is designed to train students in the field of physiotherapy and qualify them to become a physiotherapist.

15. **B.V.Sc. (Bachelor of Veterinary Science and Animal Husbandry):** B.V.Sc. is an undergraduate course that typically lasts for five years. This course is designed to train students in the field of veterinary science and animal husbandry, and qualify them to become a veterinarian.

16. **B.Sc. Environmental Science:** This is an undergraduate course that typically lasts for three years. This course is designed to provide students with an understanding of the environment, environmental issues, and the ways in which they can be addressed.

17. **B.Sc. Nutrition and Dietetics:** This is an undergraduate course that typically lasts for three years. This course is designed to provide students with an understanding of

nutrition, dietetics, and the ways in which they can be applied to promote health and wellness.

18. **B.Sc. Psychology:** This is an undergraduate course that typically lasts for three years. This course is designed to provide students with an understanding of psychology, including its theories and applications in various fields.
19. **B.Sc. Agriculture:** This is an undergraduate course that typically lasts for four years. This course is designed to train students in the field of agriculture, including the principles of crop production, soil science, and plant breeding, and qualify them
20. **B.Sc. (Bachelor of Science) in Zoology:** This is a three-year undergraduate course that covers topics related to the study of animals and their behavior, anatomy, physiology, and ecology.
21. **B.Sc. in Genetics:** This is a three-year undergraduate course that covers topics related to the study of genes and heredity, including molecular genetics, population genetics, and genetic engineering.
22. **B.Sc. in Botany:** This is a three-year undergraduate course that covers topics related to the study of plants, including their anatomy, physiology, ecology, and genetics.
23. **Bachelor of Occupational Therapy (BOT):** This is a four-year undergraduate course that focuses on the study of occupational therapy, which involves the assessment and treatment of people with physical, mental, or developmental disabilities.
24. **Bachelor of Audiology and Speech-Language Pathology (BASLP):** This is a four-year undergraduate course that focuses on the study of audiology and speech-language pathology, which involves the assessment and treatment of people with hearing, speech, or language disorders.
25. **Bachelor of Science in Medical Laboratory Technology (BSc MLT):** This is a three-year undergraduate course that

focuses on the study of laboratory medicine and diagnostic testing.

26. **Bachelor of Science in Radiology and Imaging Technology:** This is a three-year undergraduate course that focuses on the study of medical imaging techniques, including X-rays, ultrasound, and magnetic resonance imaging (MRI).

27. **Bachelor of Science in Cardiac Technology:** This is a three-year undergraduate course that focuses on the study of cardiac care and diagnostic testing, including electrocardiography (ECG), stress testing, and echocardiography.

28. **Bachelor of Science in Dialysis Technology:** This is a three-year undergraduate course that focuses on the study of dialysis and related techniques used to treat patients with kidney disease.

29. **BS in Bioinformatics:** This is an undergraduate course that combines the study of biology, computer science, and statistics. It aims to develop professionals who can apply computational and analytical tools to biological data and solve complex problems in the fields of genetics, genomics, and proteomics. The course curriculum typically includes subjects such as biology, chemistry, mathematics, computer programming, algorithms, database management, and machine learning. Graduates of this course can find employment in research and development, pharmaceuticals, biotechnology, and healthcare industries.

30. **Bachelor of Viticulture:** This is an undergraduate course that focuses on the study of grapevine cultivation and wine production. The curriculum typically includes subjects such as grapevine biology, plant pathology, soil science, wine chemistry, winemaking techniques, and marketing. Graduates of this course can find employment in the wine and viticulture industry as vineyard managers, winemakers, wine marketers, or wine analysts.

31. **Bachelor of Naturopathy and Yogic Science (BNYS):** This is an undergraduate course that combines the study of naturopathy and yoga to promote a holistic approach to healthcare. The course curriculum typically includes subjects such as anatomy and physiology, nutrition, herbal medicine, acupuncture, yoga therapy, and counseling. Graduates of this course can find employment in hospitals, wellness centers, yoga studios, and private practice as naturopathy doctors, yoga therapists, nutrition consultants, or wellness coaches.
32. **Bachelor of Unani Medicine and Surgery (BUMS):** This is an undergraduate course that focuses on the study of Unani medicine, a traditional system of medicine that originated in ancient Greece and was later developed in Persia and India. The course curriculum typically includes subjects such as Unani philosophy, anatomy and physiology, pharmacology, pathology, diagnosis, and treatment. Graduates of this course can find employment in hospitals, clinics, research institutes, and private practice as Unani doctors, health consultants, or herbal medicine practitioners.
33. BSc Courses [Multiple Specializations]: Bachelor of Science (BSc) is an undergraduate course that covers a wide range of subjects in the sciences. The course curriculum typically includes subjects such as biology, chemistry, physics, mathematics, computer science, and statistics, among others. There are many specializations available within the BSc course, such as BSc in Physics, BSc in Mathematics, BSc in Chemistry, BSc in Computer Science, and BSc in Environmental Science, among others. Graduates of these courses can find employment in research and development, education, healthcare, and other industries, depending on their specialization.

These are some of the popular courses that students from the PCB group can pursue after 12th. However, there are many other courses as well, and students can choose the one that best aligns with their interests and career goals.

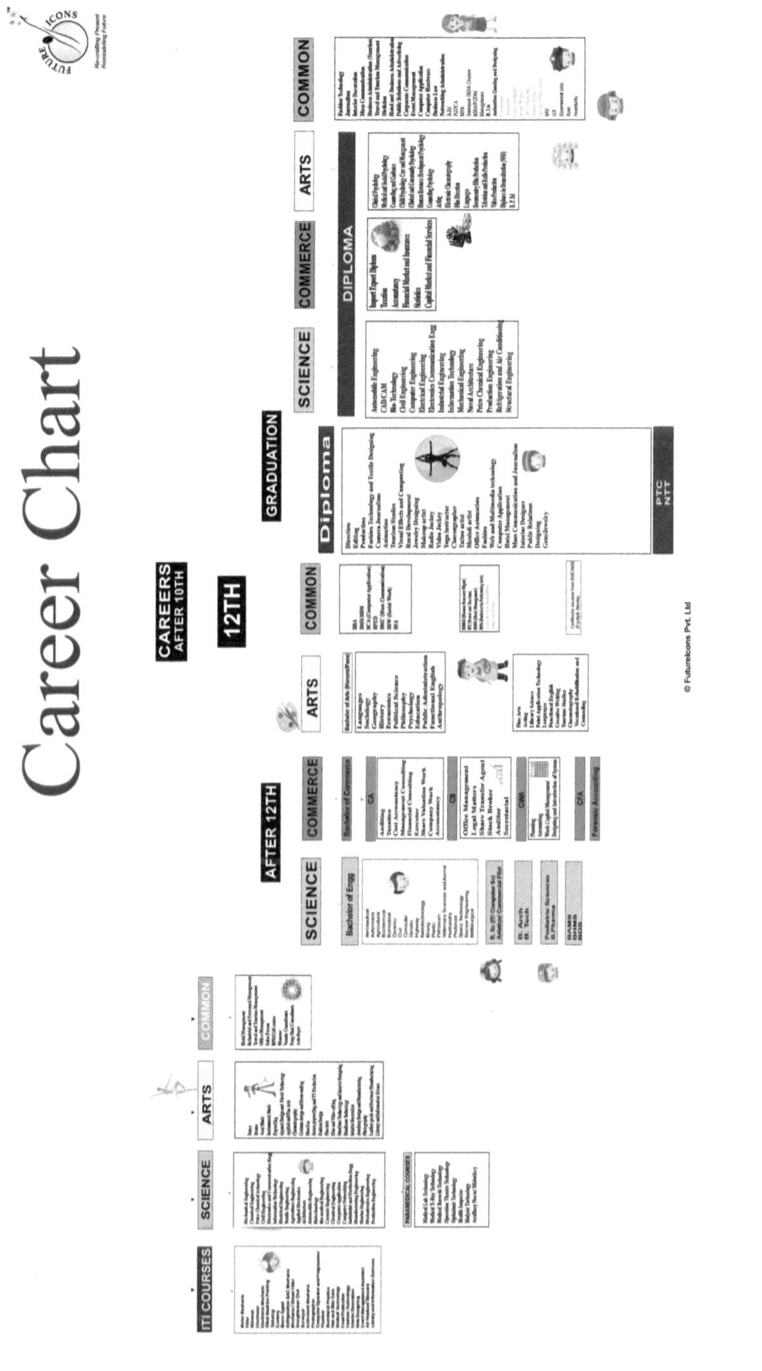

Career Chart

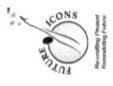

Courses for Career Options 195

Chapter 7

HIGHER EDUCATION INSTITUTES

Do you remember the time when life was a breeze? Class 10th came around, and you were just one step closer to realizing your dreams. You could enjoy life without any stress and worries. But then, as you transitioned to class 11th and 12th, things started to change. Suddenly, the pressure of choosing the right career and courses mounted on you. You found yourself searching for a purposeful career option that matched your personalilty, passion and potential.

Thankfully, you had already learned how to identify yourself in chapter 3 and map it to your career options in chapter 4. You discovered your true potential and the course options available after 12th in chapter 5. You applied the concepts from chapter 1 to solve the challenge of choosing the right course to align with your career in chapter 7.

But now, life is about to get more complex. You need to choose the right career path and course to set yourself up for a bright future. That's where higher education institutes come in. These are the stepping stones that can help you achieve your goals and dreams.

Higher education institutes come in many different forms, such as central universities, state universities, IITs, NITs, and many more. But the question remains: how can you get admission to these institutes? Well, there are several ways to do so. You can appear for national level entrance exams like CUET, JEE and NEET, state level entrance exams, institute specific entrance exams, and even merit-based admissions. Some institutes also offer management quota, foreign quota, and sponsored quota seats for admission.

How to select a higher education Institute

Your higher education institute is not just a stepping stone towards your career, but it is also a place where you will spend a significant amount of time, learn and grow as an individual, and build a strong foundation for your future. Choosing the right institute, therefore, is critical to ensure that you receive the best education and training for your chosen career.

With so many options available, it can be overwhelming to pick the right institute that aligns with your goals and aspirations. But, this is where the research comes in.

1. Identify your Self : The first step is to identify your interests and purpose in life. Think about what motivates and inspires you, and what you would like to achieve in your future career.
2. Choose a suitable career option: Once you have identified your interests and purpose, the next step is to choose a suitable career option that aligns with your goals and aspirations.
3. Map your course: After selecting a career option, the next step is to map out the course you need to take to achieve your career goals. Look for courses and programs that are relevant to your chosen career path.
4. Select an institute that aligns with your goals: Once you have mapped out your course, you need to select an institute that offers courses and programs that align with your interests and aspirations.

5. Research and explore your options: Once you have determined your goals and aspirations, research and explore your options. Look for institutes that offer courses in your field of interest and have a good reputation for delivering quality education.
6. Evaluate the faculty, curriculum, infrastructure, and campus life: When evaluating potential institutes, check the credentials and experience of the faculty, the curriculum, infrastructure, and campus life. Look for institutes that have a strong entrepreneurship cell, incubator, placement cell, collaborations with industry experts, and offer opportunities for practical training and internships.
7. Look how is the alumni placed
8. Read reviews and feedback from current and past students: Reviews and feedback from current and past students are valuable resources when evaluating potential institutes. Read reviews to understand the institute's culture and academic standards.
9. Visit the campus and interact with the faculty and students: Once you have shortlisted a few institutes, visit their campuses, attend open houses, and interact with their faculty and students. This will give you a first-hand experience of the institute's culture, facilities, and environment.
10. Consider the location and affordability: The location and affordability of an institute are important factors to consider this accounts for Parents section in your Self. Look for institutes that are easily accessible and affordable, while also providing a quality education and training.

By following these steps, you can select an institute that not only provides you with the best education and training, but also prepares you to excel in your chosen career.

Remember, your dream institute might just be waiting for you! With the right research and exploration, you can find an institute that not only provides you with the best education and training but also prepares you to excel in your chosen career. So, take the time to find the right fit, and watch as your dreams turn into reality!

Are you considering applying to a university, be it central, state, deemed, or private? Here's a general guide to help you through the admission process:

- Start by researching the universities in your desired location. Look for institutions that offer programs and courses aligned with your interests and aspirations.
- Check the eligibility criteria for admission, including academic requirements and entrance exams. For state universities, residency may also be a requirement.
- If required, apply for the entrance exam and prepare well for it.
- Fill out the application form for the desired course or program, providing accurate and complete information.Submit the required documents, including academic transcripts, entrance exam scorecards, and any other documents specified by the university.
- Pay the application fee as specified by the university to complete the application process.
- For state universities, attend the counseling session to select the course and university that best aligns with your interests and career goals.

It's important to note that specific admission criteria may vary depending on the university and the program. Therefore, make sure to carefully read the guidelines and requirements before applying. Good luck with your university admission journey!

Types of Higher Education Institutes in India and their admission criteria:

1. Central Universities

A Central University is a type of university that is established and funded by the Government of India through the Ministry of Education.to name few central universities are JNU, Delhi University, HNB Garhwal University Hyderabad University and others. Most of them have name central attached like central university of Orissa etc These universities are located in different parts of the country and offer undergraduate, postgraduate, and research programs in various fields.

To get admission in an undergraduate program in a Central University, there are several entrance exams that students can appear for, depending on the course they wish to pursue. The most common entrance exam for admission to Central Universities is the Central Universities Common Entrance Test (CUET). Generally central universities do not have state-specific reservations like state universities do. Details of CUET are given.

2. State Universities

A state university is a public university that is funded and operated by the state government. These universities are established to provide affordable and accessible higher education to residents of the state. State universities offer a wide range of undergraduate and graduate degree programs in various fields of study.

The admission process for undergraduate programs in state universities varies from state to state.

3. Private Universities & Deemed Universities

Deemed to be universities and private universities are two different types of higher education institutions in India. Deemed to be universities are institutions that were granted the status of "Deemed University" by the University Grants Commission (UGC), while private universities are institutions that are established by private organizations or individuals.

It is important to note that admission criteria may vary from one university to another, and candidates should carefully read the admission guidelines and requirements before applying.

4. Institutes of National Importance

Here is a list of some of the top Institutes of National Importance in India offering undergraduate courses, along with their admission criteria:

1. **Indian Institutes of Technology (IITs):** Admission to undergraduate programs in IITs is based on the Joint Entrance Examination (JEE) Advanced, which is conducted by the IITs on a rotational basis.
2. **Indian Institutes of Information Technology (IIITs):** Admission to undergraduate courses in IIITs is through the Joint Entrance Examination (JEE) Main, followed by the JoSAA (Joint Seat Allocation Authority) counseling process.
3. **National Institutes of Technology (NITs):** Admission to undergraduate programs in NITs is through the Joint Entrance Examination (JEE) Main, followed by the JoSAA counseling process.
4. **All India Institute of Medical Sciences (AIIMS):** Admission to undergraduate courses in AIIMS is through the AIIMS entrance exam.
5. **Indian Statistical Institute (ISI):** Admission to undergraduate courses in ISI is through the Indian Statistical Institute Admission Test (ISI-AT).
6. **National Law School of India University (NLSIU):** Admission to undergraduate courses in NLSIU is through

the Common Law Admission Test (CLAT) or the National Law School of India University Entrance Test (NLAT).
7. **Indian Institute of Science Education and Research (IISERs):** Admission to undergraduate programs in IISERs is through the Kishore Vaigyanik Protsahan Yojana (KVPY) exam or the Joint Entrance Examination (JEE) Advanced.
8. **National Institute of Fashion Technology (NIFT):** Admission to undergraduate programs in NIFT is through the NIFT Entrance Exam.
9. **Tata Institute of Social Sciences (TISS):** Admission to undergraduate courses in TISS is through the TISS National Entrance Test (TISSNET).
10. **Birla Institute of Technology and Science (BITS):** Admission to undergraduate courses in BITS is through the BITS Admission Test (BITSAT).
11. **National Institute of Design (NID):** Admission to undergraduate courses in NID is through the NID Design Aptitude Test (DAT).
12. **Indian Institutes of Management (IIMs)**

There are currently only two IIMs that offer undergraduate programs in India:

Indian Institute of Management, Indore (IIM Indore): IIM Indore offers a five-year integrated program in management (IPM) for students who have completed their 10+2 or equivalent education. The admission process includes a computer-based aptitude test (IPMAT), written ability test (WAT), and personal interview (PI).

Indian Institute of Management, Rohtak (IIM Rohtak): IIM Rohtak offers a five-year integrated program in management (IPM) for students who have completed their 10+2 or equivalent education. The admission process includes a computer-based aptitude test (IPMAT), written ability test (WAT), and personal interview (PI).

Both IIM Indore and IIM Rohtak are highly reputed institutions and offer excellent education and career opportunities for students. The admission process is rigorous and highly competitive, so it is important to prepare well for the aptitude test, WAT, and PI.

It's important to note that admission criteria may vary for each institute and program. Therefore, make sure to carefully read the guidelines and requirements before applying.

5. Pharmacy Colleges

There are numerous pharmacy colleges in India that offer undergraduate courses in pharmacy. Some of the top pharmacy colleges in India are:

- National Institute of Pharmaceutical Education and Research (NIPER)
  Courses offered: B.Pharm, M.Pharm, M.Tech (Pharm), MBA (Pharm), PhD
  Admission: Admission to undergraduate courses is through the Joint Entrance Examination (JEE) Main and admission to postgraduate courses is through the Graduate Pharmacy Aptitude Test (GPAT).

- Jamia Hamdard, New Delhi
  Courses offered: B.Pharm, D.Pharm, B.Pharm (Lateral Entry), M.Pharm, PhD
  Admission: Admission to B.Pharm is through the National Eligibility cum Entrance Test (NEET) and admission to M.Pharm is through the Graduate Pharmacy Aptitude Test (GPAT).

- University Institute of Pharmaceutical Sciences, Chandigarh

Courses offered: B.Pharm, M.Pharm, PhD
Admission: Admission to B.Pharm is through the Joint Entrance Examination (JEE) Main and admission to M.Pharm is through the Graduate Pharmacy Aptitude Test (GPAT).

- Birla Institute of Technology and Science (BITS), Pilani
  Courses offered: B.Pharm, M.Pharm, PhD
  Admission: Admission to B.Pharm is through the BITS Admission Test (BITSAT) and admission to M.Pharm is through the Graduate Pharmacy Aptitude Test (GPAT).

- Manipal College of Pharmaceutical Sciences, Karnataka
  Courses offered: B.Pharm, Pharm.D, M.Pharm, PhD
  Admission: Admission to B.Pharm is through the Manipal Entrance Test (MET) and admission to M.Pharm is through the Manipal University Online Entrance Test (MU-OET).

- Institute of Chemical Technology, Mumbai
  Courses offered: B.Pharm, M.Pharm, PhD
  Admission: Admission to B.Pharm is through the Maharashtra Common Entrance Test (MHT-CET) and admission to M.Pharm is through the Graduate Pharmacy Aptitude Test (GPAT).

Admission procedures vary for each college, but commonly used entrance exams for pharmacy colleges in India include NEET, JEE, BITSAT, MHT-CET, GPAT, and MET. Students are required to meet the eligibility criteria and clear the entrance exam to get admission to the respective college.

6. Agricultural Universities

There are several agriculture universities and colleges in India that offer undergraduate courses in various fields of agriculture. Here are some of them:

- Indian Agricultural Research Institute (IARI), New Delhi - Courses offered: B.Sc. (Hons.) Agriculture, B.Tech. (Agricultural Engineering), M.Sc. and Ph.D. in various specializations.
- Tamil Nadu Agricultural University (TNAU), Coimbatore - Courses offered: B.Sc. (Hons.) Agriculture, B.Tech. (Agricultural Engineering), B.Sc. (Hons.) Horticulture, B.F.Sc., B.Sc. (Forestry), M.Sc. and Ph.D. in various specializations.
- Punjab Agricultural University (PAU), Ludhiana - Courses offered: B.Sc. (Hons.) Agriculture, B.Tech. (Agricultural Engineering), B.Sc. (Hons.) Horticulture, B.Sc. (Hons.) Forestry, B.Sc. (Hons.) Agribusiness, M.Sc. and Ph.D. in various specializations.
- University of Agricultural Sciences (UAS), Bangalore - Courses offered: B.Sc. (Hons.) Agriculture, B.Tech. (Agricultural Engineering), B.Sc. (Hons.) Horticulture, B.F.Sc., B.Sc. (Forestry), B.Sc. (Hons.) Sericulture, M.Sc. and Ph.D. in various specializations.

To get admission to these colleges, candidates have to appear for various entrance exams conducted at the national and state levels. Some of the popular entrance exams for admission to undergraduate courses in agriculture are:

ICAR AIEEA (All India Entrance Examination for Admission)

EAMCET (Engineering, Agriculture, and Medical Common Entrance Test)

JCECE (Jharkhand Combined Entrance Competitive Examination)

BHU UET (Banaras Hindu University Undergraduate Entrance Test)

KEAM (Kerala Engineering Architecture Medical Entrance Examination)

Candidates are advised to check the official websites of the respective colleges for more details on the admission process and eligibility criteria.

7. Veterinary Colleges

There are several veterinary universities and colleges in India that offer undergraduate programs. Here are some of them:

- Guru Angad Dev Veterinary and Animal Sciences University, Ludhiana - Bachelor of Veterinary Science & Animal Husbandry (B.V.Sc. & A.H.)
- Indian Veterinary Research Institute, Bareilly - Bachelor of Veterinary Science & Animal Husbandry (B.V.Sc. & A.H.)
- Maharashtra Animal and Fishery Sciences University, Nagpur - Bachelor of Veterinary Science & Animal Husbandry (B.V.Sc. & A.H.)
- Tamil Nadu Veterinary and Animal Sciences University, Chennai - Bachelor of Veterinary Science & Animal Husbandry (B.V.Sc. & A.H.)
- West Bengal University of Animal and Fishery Sciences, Kolkata - Bachelor of Veterinary Science & Animal Husbandry (B.V.Sc. & A.H.)

Admission to these colleges is usually based on entrance exams conducted at the state or national level. Some colleges also offer admission on a merit basis. In general, students are required to have a background in science at the 10+2 level to be eligible for admission. Specific admission requirements and procedures may vary by college, so it's important to check with individual institutions for details.

8. Fine Arts Colleges

There are many fine arts universities and colleges in India. Here are some of them, along with the courses they offer at the undergraduate level and ways to get admission:

- Faculty of Fine Arts, MS University of Baroda, Vadodara, Gujarat
  Courses offered: Bachelor of Fine Arts (BFA) in Painting, Applied Arts, Sculpture, and Art History & Aesthetics
  Admission process: Entrance exam and interview

- College of Art, University of Delhi, Delhi
  Courses offered: Bachelor of Fine Arts (BFA) in Applied Art, Painting, Sculpture, and Printmaking
  Admission process: Entrance exam and interview

- Government College of Fine Arts, Chennai, Tamil Nadu
  Courses offered: Bachelor of Fine Arts (BFA) in Painting, Sculpture, and Applied Art
  Admission process: Merit-based admission

- Shantiniketan, West Bengal
  Courses offered: Bachelor of Fine Arts (BFA) in Painting, Sculpture, Graphic Art, and History of Art
  Admission process: Entrance exam and interview

- College of Fine Arts, Karnataka Chitrakala Parishath, Bangalore, Karnataka
  Courses offered: Bachelor of Fine Arts (BFA) in Painting, Applied Art, Sculpture, Graphic Art, and Art History
  Admission process: Entrance exam and interview

- Andhra University College of Fine Arts, Visakhapatnam, Andhra Pradesh
  Courses offered: Bachelor of Fine Arts (BFA) in Painting, Applied Art, Sculpture, and Photography

Admission process: Entrance exam and interview

The admission process varies from college to college, and some may also require a portfolio of your artwork or additional documentation. It's best to check the specific college's website or contact them directly for more information on their admission process.

9. Design Institutes

There are several design universities and colleges in India that offer undergraduate courses in various design specializations. Here are some of the prominent ones:

National Institute of Design (NID)

Located in Ahmedabad, NID is one of the most prestigious design colleges in India. It offers undergraduate courses in disciplines such as industrial design, communication design, textile and apparel design, and more. Admissions to NID are through the Design Aptitude Test (DAT) followed by a studio test and personal interview.

- Industrial Design Centre, IIT Bombay: The Industrial Design Centre (IDC) at the Indian Institute of Technology (IIT) Bombay offers undergraduate courses in design with specializations such as product design, interaction design, animation design, and more. Admissions are through the Undergraduate Common Entrance Examination for Design (UCEED) followed by a design aptitude test and an interview.

- Srishti Institute of Art, Design, and Technology: Srishti Institute of Art, Design, and Technology is located in Bengaluru and offers undergraduate courses in various design disciplines, including industrial design, communication design, and visual arts. Admissions are based on a Design Aptitude Test and a personal interview.

- National Institute of Fashion Technology (NIFT): NIFT is a leading design institute in India that offers undergraduate courses in fashion design, textile design, accessory design, and more. Admissions are through the NIFT Entrance Exam followed by a situation test, group discussion, and personal interview.

- MIT Institute of Design, Pune: MIT Institute of Design is located in Pune and offers undergraduate courses in industrial design, communication design, fashion design, and more. Admissions are through the Design Aptitude Test (DAT) followed by a studio test and personal interview.

- Pearl Academy, Delhi: Pearl Academy is located in Delhi and offers undergraduate courses in fashion design, product design, graphic design, and more. Admissions are through the Design Aptitude Test followed by a personal interview and a portfolio review.

There are several other design colleges in India, each with its own set of admission criteria and courses offered. Students can research the different colleges and their admission requirements before making their choice.

10. Journalism and Mass Communication Institutes

There are several universities and colleges in India that offer courses in Journalism and Mass Communication. Here are some of the top ones:

- Indian Institute of Mass Communication (IIMC), New Delhi: IIMC is one of the premier institutes in India for mass communication and journalism. It offers a Post-Graduate Diploma Course in Journalism in English, Hindi, and Urdu.

- Jamia Millia Islamia, New Delhi: Jamia Millia Islamia is a central university that offers undergraduate, postgraduate, and doctoral programs in Journalism and Mass Communication.
- Lady Shri Ram College for Women, New Delhi: LSR is a leading women's college in India that offers a Bachelor of Arts (Honours) degree in Journalism.
- Christ University, Bangalore: Christ University offers a three-year undergraduate program in Bachelor of Arts (BA) in Journalism, Psychology, and English.
- Delhi College of Arts and Commerce, New Delhi: DCAC offers a three-year undergraduate program in Bachelor of Arts (Honours) in Journalism.
- Manipal Institute of Communication, Manipal: The institute offers a three-year undergraduate program in Bachelor of Arts (BA) in Journalism and Communication.

Admission to these colleges and universities may vary depending on the institution and the course. Generally, admission is based on the performance of the student in an entrance examination, followed by an interview or group discussion. Some colleges and universities also consider academic performance in previous exams. It's best to check the official websites of the institutions for specific admission details.

11. Polytechnics

Polytechnic education in India is typically offered by institutions that are recognized by the All India Council for Technical Education (AICTE) and the respective State Boards of Technical Education. Here are some popular Polytechnic colleges in India:

- Government Polytechnic, Mumbai: Offers diploma courses in Civil, Electrical, Mechanical, and Electronics Engineering, among others. Admission is based on merit in the qualifying exam.

- Delhi Institute of Tool Engineering: Offers diploma courses in Tool and Die Making, Mechatronics, and Production Engineering, among others. Admission is based on merit in the qualifying exam.
- Government Polytechnic, Pune: Offers diploma courses in Civil, Mechanical, and Electronics Engineering, among others. Admission is based on merit in the qualifying exam.
- Government Polytechnic, Lucknow: Offers diploma courses in Civil, Electrical, Mechanical, and Electronics Engineering, among others. Admission is based on merit in the qualifying exam.
- Government Polytechnic, Nagpur: Offers diploma courses in Civil, Electrical, Mechanical, and Electronics Engineering, among others. Admission is based on merit in the qualifying exam.
- Government Polytechnic College, Chennai: Offers diploma courses in Civil, Mechanical, and Electrical Engineering, among others. Admission is based on merit in the qualifying exam.
- KJ Somaiya Polytechnic, Mumbai: Offers diploma courses in Electronics, Mechanical, and Computer Engineering, among others. Admission is based on merit in the qualifying exam.
- CIPET (Central Institute of Plastics Engineering and Technology), Chennai: Offers diploma courses in Plastics Technology, Manufacturing Technology, and CAD/CAM, among others. Admission is based on merit in the qualifying exam.

The admission process for most Polytechnic courses in India is based on merit in the qualifying exam. Candidates are required to fulfill the eligibility criteria, which typically include passing Class 10 or equivalent with a minimum percentage. Some institutions may also conduct their own entrance tests for admission.

Exams to get admission in Undergraduate program

1. Central Universities is the Central Universities Common Entrance Test (CUET)

CUET is conducted once a year, usually in the month of May or June, by a consortium of Central Universities. The test is conducted in online mode and consists of multiple-choice questions from different subjects, including English, General Awareness, and the subject related to the course the student wishes to pursue.

Apart from CUET, some Central Universities may also have their own entrance exams for admission to their undergraduate programs. For instance, Jawaharlal Nehru University (JNU) conducts its own entrance exam called JNU Entrance Exam (JNUEE).

To be eligible for admission to an undergraduate program in a Central University, a student must have completed their 10+2 or an equivalent examination from a recognized board. The minimum percentage requirement may vary for different courses and universities.

In addition to CUET or the university-specific entrance exams, some Central Universities may also consider the marks obtained by the student in their 10+2 or equivalent examination. Students who meet the eligibility criteria and clear the entrance exams are called for counseling and seat allocation. Apart from central Universities few state universities , private universities and deemed to be universities participate in CUET and take admissions through CUET. Below is the list of Universities that participate in CUET

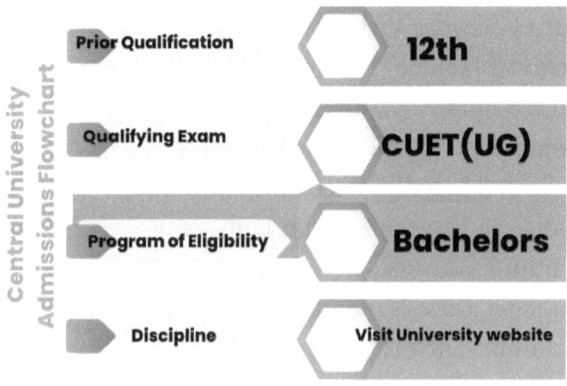

Central Universities That Participate In CUET

1. Aligarh Muslim University
2. Assam University
3. Babasaheb Bhimrao Ambedkar University
4. Banaras Hindu University
5. Central Sanskrit University
6. Central Tribal University Of Andhra Pradesh
7. Central University Of Andhra Pradesh
8. Central University Of Gujarat
9. Central University Of Haryana
10. Central University Of Himachal Pradesh
11. Central University Of Jammu
12. Central University Of Jharkhand
13. Central University Of Karnataka
14. Central University Of Kashmir
15. Central University Of Kerala
16. Central University Of Odisha
17. Central University Of Rajasthan
18. Central University Of South Bihar
19. Central University Of Tamil Nadu

20. Dr. Harisingh Gour Vishwavidyalaya
21. Guru Ghasidas Vishwavidyalaya
22. Hemvati Nandan Bahuguna Garhwal University
23. Indira Gandhi National Tribal University
24. Jawaharlal Nehru University
25. Mahatma Gandhi Antarrashtriya Hindi Vishwavidyalaya
26. Mahatma Gandhi Central University
27. Manipur University
28. Maulana Azad National Urdu University
29. Mizoram University
30. Nagaland University
31. National Sanskrit University
32. North-Eastern Hill University
33. Pondicherry University
34. Rajiv Gandhi University
35. Shri Lal Bahadur Shastri National Sanskrit University
36. Sikkim University
37. Tezpur University
38. The English And Foreign Languages University
39. Tripura University
40. University Of Allahabad
41. University Of Delhi
42. University Of Hyderabad
43. Visva-Bharati University

State Universities

44. Barkatullah University
45. Cluster University Of Jammu
46. Cluster University Of Srinagar
47. Delhi Skill And Entrepreneurship University
48. Devi Ahilya Vishwavidyalaya
49. Dr. A.P.J. Abdul Kalam Technical University
50. Dr. B.R. Ambedkar School Of Economics University

51. Dr. B.R. Ambedkar University Delhi
52. Govt. College For Women, Parade Ground, Jammu
53. Guru Gobind Singh Indraprastha University
54. Harcourt Butler Technical University, Kanpur
55. Indira Gandhi Delhi Technical University For Women
56. Islamia College Of Science And Commerce
57. Jharkhand Raksha Shakti University
58. Madan Mohan Malaviya University Of Technology
59. Mahatma Jyotiba Phule Rohilkhand University
60. Sardar Patel University Of Police Security And Criminal Justice
61. Shri Mata Vaishno Devi University
62. University Of Jammu
63. Vikram University

Deemed To Be Universities Listed In Cuet

64. Avinashilingam Institute For Home Science And Higher Education For Women
65. Chinmaya Vishwavidyapeeth
66. Dayalbagh Educational Institute
67. Footwear Design And Development Institute
68. Gujarat Vidyapith
69. Gurukula Kangri
70. Lakshmibai National Institute Of Physical Education
71. Manav Rachna International Institute Of Research And Studies
72. Ramakrishna Mission Vivekananda Educational And Research Institute
73. Shobhit University
74. Tata Institute Of Social Sciences (Tiss)
75. The Gandhigram Rural Institute (Dtbu)

Private Universities That Participate In Cuet

76. Apeejay Stya University
77. Apex University
78. Arunachal University Of Studies
79. Asbm University
80. Bahra University (Shimla Hills)
81. Bml Munjal University
82. Career Point University
83. Chanakya University
84. Chhatrapati Shivaji Maharaj University
85. G D Goenka University
86. Galgotias University
87. Geeta University, Panipat, Delhi-Ncr, Haryana
88. Gla University Mathura
89. Himalayan University Itanagar
90. Ies University
91. Iilm University, Greater Noida
92. Iilm University, Gurugram
93. Iimt University
94. Invertis University
95. Itm University Gwalior
96. Jagan Nath University Bahadurgarh Haryana
97. Jagannath University, Jaipur (Rajasthan)
98. Jaypee University Of Information Technology
99. K.R. Mangalam University
100. Lovely Professional University
101. Manav Rachna University
102. Mangalayatan University Jabalpur
103. Mangalayatan University, Aligarh
104. Mewar University
105. Mody University Of Science And Technology
106. Nicmar University, Pune
107. NIIT University

108. Nirwan University, Jaipur
109. Noida International University
110. Rnb Global University
111. Sangam University
112. Sanskriti University
113. Sharda University
114. Shoolini University
115. Sikkim Professional University
116. SRM University
117. Suresh Gyan Vihar University Jaipur
118. Teerthanker Mahaveer University
119. The Icfai University, Jaipur
120. Upes - Dehradun
121. Usha Martin University
122. Vivekananda Global University

2. Joint Entrance Exam (JEE)

The Joint Entrance Examination (JEE) is one of the most competitive engineering entrance exams in India. It is conducted by the National Testing Agency (NTA) for admission to undergraduate engineering and architecture courses at prestigious institutes such as the Indian Institutes of Technology (IITs), National Institutes of Technology (NITs), and other centrally funded technical institutes.

The JEE exam is divided into two parts: JEE Main and JEE Advanced. JEE Main is conducted twice a year in January and April, while JEE Advanced is held once a year in May. The exam consists of multiple-choice questions that test the candidate's knowledge in physics, chemistry, and mathematics.

Institutes that take admission through JEE include:

1. Indian Institutes of Technology (IITs)
2. National Institutes of Technology (NITs)

3. Indian Institutes of Information Technology (IIITs)
4. Centrally Funded Technical Institutes (CFTIs)
5. Schools of Planning and Architecture (SPAs)

AIEEE (All India Engineering Entrance Examination) has been replaced by JEE Main. It is no longer conducted as a separate exam. JEE Main serves as the entrance exam for NITs, IIITs, and other CFTIs.

The tentative date for the JEE Main exam is usually announced in December or January, with the exam typically held in February or March for the first session and in April for the second session. The application forms for the JEE Main exam are usually released a few months before the exam date.

To get admission in engineering or architecture through JEE, students must first qualify for JEE Main. Those who score high in JEE Main are eligible to appear for JEE Advanced, which is required for admission to the IITs. After the JEE Advanced exam, students who score well are eligible for admission to the IITs. Students who qualify in JEE Main can also get admission in NITs, IIITs, and other CFTIs. To get admission in SPA, a candidate must qualify in the JEE Main Paper 2 or NATA (National Aptitude Test in Architecture).

In conclusion, JEE is a highly competitive entrance exam that opens up a wide range of opportunities for students to pursue their engineering or architecture dreams. To succeed in the exam, students must prepare thoroughly and practice consistently. Good luck to all the aspiring engineers and architects out there!

3. National Eligibility cum Entrance Test (NEET)

The National Eligibility cum Entrance Test (NEET) is an entrance exam conducted by the National Testing Agency (NTA) for admission to undergraduate medical and dental courses in India.

The exam is highly competitive and is required for admission to prestigious medical and dental colleges across the country.

Institutes that take admission through NEET include:

i. All India Institutes of Medical Sciences (AIIMS)
ii. Jawaharlal Institute of Postgraduate Medical Education and Research (JIPMER)
iii. Armed Forces Medical College (AFMC)
iv. Government and Private Medical and Dental Colleges in India

NEET helps students get admission into medical and dental courses such as MBBS, BDS, BHMS, BAMS, and other allied health sciences courses.

The tentative date for the NEET exam is usually announced in December or January, with the exam typically held in May. The application forms for the NEET exam are usually released a few months before the exam date.

NEET is a highly competitive exam that requires extensive preparation and dedication. The exam consists of 180 multiple-choice questions that test the candidate's knowledge in physics, chemistry, and biology.

To get admission in medical courses through NEET, students must first qualify for the exam. After qualifying in the exam, students must apply for counseling to get admission in medical or dental colleges based on their rank and availability of seats. Counseling is conducted by the Directorate General of Health Services (DGHS) for the 15% All India Quota seats and by the respective state authorities for the remaining 85% state quota seats.

In conclusion, NEET is a crucial exam for students who aspire to become medical professionals. To succeed in the exam, students must prepare thoroughly and practice consistently.

4. National Aptitude Test in Architecture (NATA)

The National Aptitude Test in Architecture (NATA) is a national-level entrance exam conducted by the Council of Architecture (COA) for admission to undergraduate architecture programs in India. NATA measures the candidate's aptitude and skills required for a career in architecture.

NATA has two parts: Part A and Part B. Part A is a computer-based test that tests the candidate's mathematical, general aptitude, and drawing skills. Part B is a drawing test that is conducted on a sheet of paper.

The following are the important details regarding the NATA exam:

a. The application process for NATA is completely online.
b. The application process usually starts in January and ends in March.
c. NATA is conducted twice a year, usually in April and July.
d. The exam is conducted in two parts - Part A and Part B.
   i. Part A consists of 60 multiple-choice questions, which are divided into two sections - Mathematics and General Aptitude.
   ii. Part B consists of two questions that test the candidate's drawing skills.
e. The NATA scorecard is valid for one year.
f. The candidate needs to apply for admission to the respective colleges they wish to join.

The admission process for architecture courses varies from college to college. Some colleges conduct their own entrance exams, while others consider NATA scores for admission.

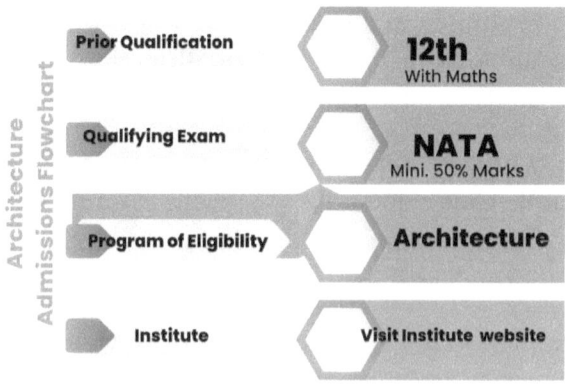

5. Common Law Admission Test (CLAT)

The Common Law Admission Test (CLAT) is a national-level entrance exam conducted in India for admission to undergraduate and postgraduate law programmes offered by various law colleges and universities in India. It is conducted by the Consortium of National Law Universities (NLUs) on a rotational basis.

CLAT is a computer-based test, and it assesses a candidate's proficiency in English language, logical reasoning, legal aptitude, quantitative aptitude, and general awareness. The exam is typically held in the month of May or June, and the application process usually starts in January or February.

The undergraduate programme offered through CLAT is a five-year integrated law programme, while the postgraduate programme is a one-year LLM course. The participating institutes for CLAT include NLUs like NLSIU Bangalore, NALSAR Hyderabad, NLIU Bhopal, WBNUJS Kolkata, and many others.

The eligibility criteria for the undergraduate programme is that the candidate should have passed 10+2 or an equivalent exam with a minimum of 45% marks (40% for SC/ST candidates). For the postgraduate programme, the candidate should have completed a three-year LLB or five-year integrated LLB programme with a minimum of 50% marks (45% for SC/ST candidates).

The exam duration for CLAT is two hours, and it consists of 150 multiple-choice questions. The exam has negative marking, with one-fourth of a mark deducted for each incorrect answer. The exam is conducted in English medium.

Overall, CLAT is a highly competitive exam and requires a lot of preparation and practice to crack. Candidates interested in pursuing law as a career can consider appearing for the exam and targeting the participating institutes to further their legal education.

6. National Institute of Fashion Technology Entrance Exam (NIFT Entrance Exam)

The National Institute of Fashion Technology (NIFT) conducts an entrance exam every year for admission to its undergraduate courses. The exam is usually held in the month of January or February. The exact date of the exam is announced by NIFT on its official website.

As for the availability of forms, the NIFT entrance exam application forms are generally released in the month of October or November. The application process is online, and candidates can submit their forms by visiting the official website of NIFT.

The NIFT entrance exam is conducted for admission to various undergraduate courses in fashion and design. Some of the popular courses that NIFT offers admission to through this entrance exam include:

- Bachelor of Design (B.Des) in Fashion Design
- Bachelor of Design (B.Des) in Leather Design
- Bachelor of Design (B.Des) in Accessory Design
- Bachelor of Design (B.Des) in Textile Design
- Bachelor of Design (B.Des) in Knitwear Design
- Bachelor of Design (B.Des) in Fashion Communication

The NIFT entrance exam is a highly competitive exam, and thousands of students across the country appear for it every year. The exam consists of two parts - a written test and a situation test. The written test assesses the candidate's aptitude for design, while the situation test evaluates their ability to come up with innovative solutions to given design problems.

7. National Institute of Design Entrance Exam (NID Entrance Exam) –

The National Institute of Design Entrance Exam (NID Entrance Exam) for undergraduate courses is a highly sought-after exam that is conducted every year. The exam is held in the month of January, and the exact date is usually announced on the official website of the institute.

As far as the availability of forms is concerned, the application process for the NID Entrance Exam usually begins in the month of October or November. Interested candidates can access the application form on the official website of NID, and the last date for submitting the form is usually in December.

The NID Entrance Exam is conducted for admission to undergraduate courses in design, which include the following:

- Bachelor of Design (B.Des.)
- Graduate Diploma Program in Design (GDPD)

The exam is conducted in two stages - the first stage is a written test, which is followed by a studio test and an interview. The written test is designed to assess the candidate's knowledge in areas such as design aptitude, visual perception, and communication skills.

Overall, the NID Entrance Exam is a crucial step for students who wish to pursue a career in design. By staying updated on the exam schedule and application process, students can increase their chances of getting admission to this prestigious institute.

8. Indian Maritime University Common Entrance Test (IMU CET)

The Indian Maritime University Common Entrance Test (IMU CET) is a national level exam conducted for admission to undergraduate courses in maritime studies. The exam is conducted by the Indian Maritime University (IMU) every year.

The courses offered through IMU CET for undergraduate students include:

- B.Tech in Marine Engineering
- B.Tech in Naval Architecture and Ocean Engineering
- B.Sc. in Nautical Science
- Diploma in Nautical Science (DNS)

The exam is typically held in the month of June, and the exact date for the exam is announced on the official website of IMU. The application process for IMU CET usually begins in the month of April, and interested candidates can access the application form on the official website.

The application form can be filled online, and candidates need to provide their personal and academic details, along with relevant documents and application fee. The last date for submitting the application form is usually in May.

The IMU CET exam is conducted in an online mode, and the question paper is divided into six sections, namely, English, general knowledge, general aptitude, mathematics, physics, and chemistry. The total duration of the exam is three hours.

Overall, IMU CET is a crucial step for students who wish to pursue a career in the maritime industry. By staying updated on the exam schedule and application process, students can increase their chances of getting admission to this prestigious university.

9. Indian Institute of Crafts and Design Entrance Exam (IICD Entrance Exam)

The Indian Institute of Crafts and Design (IICD) is a premier institute that offers undergraduate and postgraduate courses in various fields of design. The IICD Entrance Exam is conducted every year for admission to undergraduate courses, which are highly sought after by students who are interested in pursuing a career in design.

The IICD Entrance Exam is usually held in the month of May or June. The exact date is usually announced on the official website of the institute. The application process for the exam begins in the month of March or April, and interested candidates can access the application form on the official website of IICD.

The courses offered by IICD are as follows:

- Bachelor of Design (B.Des.) in Crafts and Design - 4 years
- Bachelor of Vocation (B.Voc.) in Crafts and Design - 3 years

The B.Des. program is a four-year course that is designed to provide students with a comprehensive understanding of various crafts and design techniques. The course curriculum includes subjects such as textiles, pottery, metalwork, and woodwork, among others.

The B.Voc. program, on the other hand, is a three-year course that is aimed at providing students with hands-on training in specific crafts and design skills. The course curriculum includes a mix of theory and practical training, and the focus is on developing skills that are relevant to the industry.

Overall, the IICD Entrance Exam is a crucial step for students who wish to pursue a career in design. By staying updated on the exam schedule and application process, students can increase their chances of getting admission to this prestigious institute.

10. All India Hotel Management Entrance Examination (AIHMCT)

The All India Hotel Management Entrance Examination (AIHMEE) is a national level entrance exam conducted for admission to undergraduate courses in the field of Hotel Management. The exam is conducted by the National Council for Hotel Management and Catering Technology (NCHMCT).

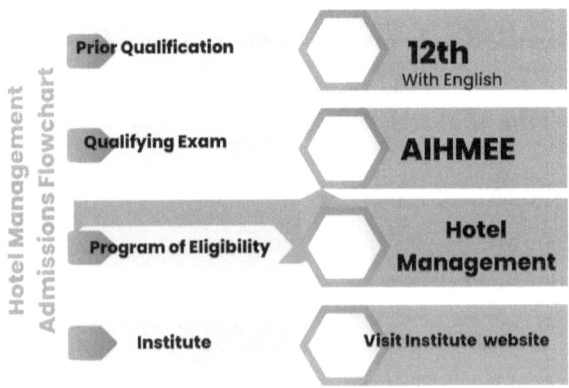

The AIHMEE exam is conducted for admission to the following undergraduate courses:

- Bachelor of Science (B.Sc.) in Hospitality and Hotel Administration
- Diploma in Food Production
- Diploma in Bakery and Confectionery

The AIHMEE exam is usually conducted in the month of April every year. The exact date of the exam is usually announced on the official website of NCHMCT. The application process for the AIHMEE exam usually begins in the month of December or January. Interested candidates can access the application form on the official website of NCHMCT, and the last date for submitting the form is usually in March.

The AIHMEE exam is a computer-based test that consists of multiple-choice questions. The exam consists of 200 questions that are divided into five sections, namely, Numerical Ability and Scientific Aptitude, Reasoning and Logical Deduction, General Knowledge and Current Affairs, English Language, and Aptitude for Service Sector.

Well, there you have it! We've covered a lot of ground on career coaching for class 12 students. But, if you feel like you still need more information, don't worry, we've got you covered! Our career coaching programs, under the name "Prabodhan", meaning enlightenment, are conducted online, one-to-one, and in schools. We have helped countless students achieve their dreams by guiding them towards the right career path. And if you want to stay updated on the latest career-related news, trends, and insights, be sure to check out our website at www.futureicons.co.in. We wish you all the best in your career journey!